Read-Aloud Anthology
Kindergarten

 Harcourt

Orlando   Boston   Dallas   Chicago   San Diego

Visit *The Learning Site!*

www.harcourtschool.com

For permission to reprint copyrighted material, grateful acknowledgment is made to the following sources:

Agathon Press, New York: "Aiken Drum" from *Teaching the Young Child* by Susan Rounds. Lyrics and music © 1975 by Susan Rounds.
Boyds Mills Press: "The Tortoise and the Hare" from *The Children's Aesop*, retold by Stephanie Calmenson. Text copyright 1988 by Doubleday Book & Music Clubs, Inc.
Ruth Cohen, Inc., on behalf of Patrick J. Gallagher, Executor: *Chicken Forgets* by Miska Miles. Text copyright © 1976 by Miska Miles. Published by Little, Brown and Company.
The Lois Lenski Covey Foundation, Inc.: "Sing a Song of People" from *The Life I Live* by Lois Lenski. Text copyright © 1965 by The Lois Lenski Covey Foundation, Inc.
Harry B. Coyle: English lyrics from "The Elephant Song" (Retitled: "The Elephants") in *A Chorus of Cultures* by Alma Flor Ada, Violet J. Harris, and Lee Bennett Hopkins. Lyrics copyright © 1983 by Deborah K. Coyle (1932-1995).
 Crown Publishers, Inc.: *Mother, Mother, I Want Another* by Maria Polushkin, illustrated by Diane Dawson. Text copyright © 1978 by Maria Polushkin; illustrations copyright © 1978 by Diane Dawson.
Dutton Children's Books, a division of Penguin Putnam Inc.: "Buenos días/Good Morning" from *De Colores and Other Latin-American Folk Songs for Children* by José-Luis Orozco. Lyrics and music copyright © 1994 by José-Luis Orozco.
Ell-Bern Publishing Company (ASCAP), 1844 N. Mohawk, Chicago, IL 60614: Lyrics and music from "You'll Sing a Song and I'll Sing a Song" by Ella Jenkins. Lyrics and music copyright © 1966, assigned 1968 to Ella Jenkins.
Flint Public Library, 1026 E. Kearsley St., Flint, MI 48502: "Quack! Quack! Quack!" and "Five Little Pigs" from *Ring a Ring o' Roses: Finger Plays for Preschool Children.*
Folkways Music Publishers, Inc., New York, NY: From "All Work Together" by Woody Guthrie. TRO - © copyright 1956 (renewed) 1963 (renewed) by Folkways Music Publishers, Inc.
 Greenwillow Books, a division of William Morrow & Company, Inc.: "The Strongest One of All" from *Merry-Go-Round: Four Stories* by Mirra Ginsburg, illustrated by Jose Aruego and Ariane Dewey. Text copyright © 1969, 1973, 1977, 1981 by Mirra Ginsburg; illustrations copyright © 1977, 1981, 1992 by Jose Aruego and Ariane Dewey. Music from "If You're Happy and You Know It" by Nicki Weiss. Music copyright © 1987 by John Krumich.
Groundwood Books/Douglas & McIntyre: *Emily's House* by Niko Scharer, illustrated by Joanne Fitzgerald. Text copyright © 1990 by Niko Scharer; illustrations copyright © 1990 by Joanne Fitzgerald.
The Hampton-Brown Company: Spanish lyrics from "The Elephant Song" (Retitled: "The Elephants") in *A Chorus of Cultures: Developing Literacy Through Multicultural Poetry* by Alma Flor Ada, Violet J. Harris, and Lee Bennett Hopkins. Spanish lyrics copyright © 1993 by Hampton-Brown Books.
Harcourt Brace & Company: "Fireflies, Fireflies" and "Little Silk Worms" from *Dragon Kites and Dragonflies* by Demi Hitz. Text copyright © 1986 by Demi. "Mr. Backward" and illustration from *Bing Bang Boing* by Douglas Florian. Copyright © 1994 by Douglas Florian. "Yellow Butter" from *The Llama Who Had No Pajama: 100 Favorite Poems* by Mary Ann Hoberman. Text copyright © 1981 by Mary Ann Hoberman.
HarperCollins Publishers: "Tommy" from *Bronzeville Boys and Girls* by Gwendolyn Brooks. Text copyright © 1956 by Gwendolyn Brooks Blakely. "The Fish with the Deep Sea Smile" from *Nibble Nibble* by Margaret Wise Brown. Text copyright © 1959 by William R. Scott, Inc., renewed 1987 by Roberta Brown Rauch. *The Seashore Noisy Book* by Margaret Wise Brown. Text copyright © 1941 by Margaret Wise Brown. "Little Seeds" from *The Winds That Come From Far Away* by Else Holmelund Minarik, illustrated by Joan Phyllis Berg. Text copyright © 1964 by Else Holmelund Minarik; illustrations copyright © 1964 by Joan Phyllis Berg. "The Three Bears," "The Gingerbread Man," "The Three Little Pigs," "The Lion and the Mouse," and "The Shoemaker and the Elves" from *The Three Bears & 15 Other Stories* by Anne Rockwell. Text copyright © 1975 by Anne Rockwell. "Bear in There" and "Blame" from *A Light in the Attic* by Shel Silverstein. Copyright © 1981 by Evil Eye Music, Inc. *Caps for Sale* by Esphyr Slobodkina. Copyright © 1940 and 1947, © renewed 1968 by Esphyr Slobodkina.
Elizabeth Hauser: "Dogs" from *Around and About* by Marchette Chute. Text copyright 1957 by E. P. Dutton; text copyright renewed 1985 by Marchette Chute.
Homeland Publishing (CAPAC), a division of Troubadour Records Ltd.: "Everything Grows" by Raffi and D. Pike, music by Raffi from *Raffi's Top 10 Songs to Read* by Raffi. © 1987 by Homeland Publishing (CAPAC), a division of Troubadour Records Ltd. "Down by the Bay" from *Singable Songs for the Very Young* by Raffi (1976). "Wheels on the Bus" (Retitled: "The Bus Song") from *Rise and Shine* by Raffi (1982).
Houghton Mifflin Company: From *Jamaica's Find* by Juanita Havill, illustrated by Anne Sibley O'Brien. Text copyright © 1986 by Juanita Havill; illustrations copyright © 1986 by Anne Sibley O'Brien.
Kids Can Press Ltd., Toronto, Canada: *Franklin in the Dark* by Paulette Bourgeois, illustrated by Brenda Clark. Text copyright © 1986 by P. B. Creations Inc.; illustrations copyright © 1986 by Brenda Clark Illustrator Inc. Franklin is a trademark of Kids Can Press Ltd.
Hal Leonard Corporation: "Wild Geese" from *Children's Songs from Japan* by F. White and K. Akiyama. Lyrics and music copyright © 1960 by Edward B. Marks Music Company; lyrics and music copyright renewed. International copyright secured.
Lothrop, Lee & Shepard Books, a division of William Morrow & Company, Inc.: *Grandfather and I* by Helen E. Buckley, illustrated by Jan Ormerod. Text copyright © 1994 by Helen E. Buckley; illustrations copyright © 1994 by Jan Ormerod. Music from "The Farmer in the Dell," "Bingo," "The Mulberry Bush," and "The Bear Went Over the Mountain" from *Singing Bee! A Collection of Favorite Children's Songs*, compiled by Jane Hart. Music copyright © 1982 by Jane Hart.
Ludlow Music, Inc., New York: "Mary Was a Red Bird" ("Mary Wore Her Red Dress") collected, adapted, and arranged by Alan Lomax and John A. Lomax. Lyrics and music TRO - © copyright 1941 (renewed) by Ludlow Music, Inc.
Mariposa Printing & Publishing, Inc.: "Coyote & Turtle" from *Coyote & …: Native American Folk Tales*, retold by Joe Hayes. Text copyright © 1983 by Joe Hayes.
McClelland & Stewart Inc., The Canadian Publishers: "The Ants Came Marching," musical arrangement by Keith MacMillan from *Sally Go Round the Sun* by Edith Fowke. Copyright © 1969 by McClelland and Stewart, Inc.
Morrow Junior Books, a division of William Morrow & Company, Inc.: *A House by the Sea* by Joanne Ryder, illustrated by Melissa Sweet. Text copyright © 1994 by Joanne Ryder; illustrations copyright © 1994 by Melissa Sweet.
Music Sales Corporation (ASCAP): "Kookaburra Sits in the Old Gumtree" by Marion Sinclair. Lyrics and music copyright © 1934, renewed by Larrikin Music Publishing Pty Ltd. International copyright secured.
Anita E. Posey: "When All the World's Asleep" by Anita E. Posey from *Rings and Things*. Published by Macmillan Publishing Company, 1967.
G. P. Putnam's Sons, a division of Penguin Putnam Inc.: From *The Rooster Who Went to His Uncle's Wedding* by Alma Flor Ada, illustrated by Kathleen Kuchera. Text copyright © 1993 by Alma Flor Ada; illustrations copyright © 1993 by Kathleen Kuchera. *The Town Mouse and the Country Mouse* by Lorinda Bryan Cauley. Text copyright © 1984 by Lorinda Bryan Cauley.
Marian Reiner, on behalf of Beatrice Schenk de Regniers: "Keep a Poem in Your Pocket" and slightly adapted from "What Did You Put in Your Pocket?" in *Something Special* by Beatrice Schenk de Regniers. Text copyright © 1958, 1986 by Beatrice Schenk de Regniers.
Sidney Robertson, collector: "Bought Me a Cat."
Scholastic Inc.: *Stone Soup* by Ann McGovern. Text copyright © 1968 by Ann McGovern.
Charles Scribner's Sons, an imprint of Macmillan Publishing Company: "If You Ever" from *The Poetry Troupe*, compiled by Isabel Wilner. Published by Charles Scribner's Sons, 1977.
The Family of Ruth Crawford Seeger: Music from "Old Mister Rabbit" in *American Folk Songs for Children* by Ruth Crawford Seeger. Music copyright 1948 by Ruth Crawford Seeger. Published by Doubleday (still in print, 1998).
Trails West Publishing: *The Terrible Tragadabas* by Joe Hayes. Text copyright © 1987 by Joe Hayes.
Viking Kestrel, a division of Penguin Putnam Inc.: From *Let's Go, Froggy!* by Jonathan London, illustrated by Frank Remkiewicz. Text copyright © 1994 by Jonathan London, illustrations copyright © 1994 by Frank Remkiewicz.
Warren-Mattox Productions: Music and lyrics from "Loop de Loo" in *Shake It to the One That You Love the Best*, adapted by Cheryl Warren Mattox. Copyright © 1989 by Warren-Mattox Productions.
The H. W. Wilson Company: "Henny Penny," "Counting Crocodiles," "The Fearsome Beast," and "Rattlesnake, Mouse, and Coyote" from *The Flannel Board Storytelling Book* by Judy Sierra. Text copyright © 1987 by Judy Sierra.

8 9 10 11 12 13 14 15 076 10 09 08 07 06 05 04 03 02

Contents

Stories

Songs

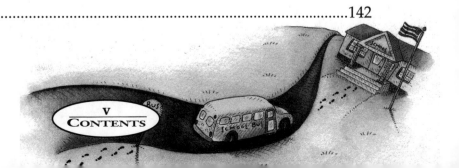

Reading Aloud to Children

by Dr. Dorothy S. Strickland

Read to children daily! Read with enthusiasm! Read a story or poem more than once, and get children thinking and talking about it: How did the fox trick the gingerbread boy? Were you surprised that the tortoise beat the hare in the race? How did that poet make you laugh?

Reading aloud to children is a part of every teacher's repertoire of "absolute musts." When children hear a poem like "If You Ever" or "The Fish with the Deep Sea Smile," they hear the beauty and rhythm of our language spoken aloud, while also building their background knowledge about ocean life. When they sing the cumulative verses of a silly song like "There's a Hole in the Middle of the Sea," they are playing with the meaning, sequence, and sounds of words; not surprisingly, this spills over into their own writing, speech, and dramatic play.

Sharing literature with children increases their vocabulary and their understanding of how the language "works." Poems and stories are full of sentence structures outside of ordinary speech—interesting ways to describe, to compare, and to contrast, such as "the little wee bear" and "the great big bear." Children unconsciously incorporate these models into their own thoughts and speech.

The more exposure children have to a variety of literary forms, the easier it is for them to understand literature. Fables, such as "The Lion and the Mouse," and story elements, such as the contrast between good and evil in "The Three Billy-Goats Gruff," are basic literary components that children will meet over and over again throughout life.

The benefits from reading aloud to children are deep and abiding. Lucky is the child with whom it is done frequently and well.

Keep a

POEM

in Your Pocket

Keep a poem in your pocket
and a picture in your head
and you'll never feel lonely
at night when you're in bed.

The little poem will sing to you
the little picture bring to you
a dozen dreams to dance to you
at night when you're in bed.

So—
Keep a picture in your pocket
and a poem in your head
and you'll never feel lonely
at night when you're in bed.

Beatrice Schenk de Regniers

Dogs

The dogs I know
Have many shapes.
For some are big and tall,
And some are long,
And
some
are thin,
And some are fat and small.

And some are little bits of fluff
And have no shape at all.

Marchette Chute

Pease Porridge

Pease porridge hot,
Pease porridge cold,
Pease porridge in the pot
Nine days old.

Some like it hot,
Some like it cold,
Some like it in the pot
Nine days old.

Mother Goose

Dig a Little Hole

a finger play

Dig a little hole, *(Dig.)*
Plant a little seed, *(Drop seed.)*
Pour a little water, *(Pour.)*
Pull a little weed. *(Pull up and throw away.)*

Chase a little bug— *(Make chasing motions with hands.)*
Heigh-ho, there he goes! *(Shade eyes.)*
Give a little sunshine, *(Cup hands, lift to the sun.)*
Grow a little rose. *(Smell flower, smiling.)*

Peter Piper

Peter Piper picked a peck of pickled peppers.
Did Peter Piper pick a peck of pickled peppers?
If Peter Piper picked a peck of pickled peppers,
Where's the peck of pickled peppers that
    Peter Piper picked?

Mother Goose

Five Little Pigs

This little pig makes an "oink, oink" sound,
This little pig is fat and round.
This little pig roots all around,
With his piggy snout, he digs up the ground.
This little piggy has a curly tail.
He eats his lunch from a shiny pail.
This little piggy doesn't seem to care
If any of the other pigs get their share.

QUACK! QUACK! QUACK!

a finger play

Five little ducks that I once knew, (*Hold up five fingers.*)
Big ones, little ones, skinny ones too,
But the one little duck with the
Feather on his back, (*Hold up one finger.*)
All he could do was, "Quack, Quack, Quack."
(*Make quacking motions with thumb and four fingers.*)
All he could do was, "Quack, Quack, Quack."

Down to the river they would go,
Waddling, waddling to and fro, (*waddling motions*)
But the one little duck with the
Feather on his back, (*Hold up one finger.*)
All he could do was, "Quack, Quack, Quack."
All he could do was, "Quack, Quack, Quack."

Up from the river they would come.
Ho, Ho, Ho, Ho, Hum, Hum, Hum.
But the one little duck with the
Feather on his back, (*Hold up one finger.*)
All he could do was, "Quack, Quack, Quack."
All he could do was, "Quack, Quack, Quack."

The Cat and the Fiddle

Hey, diddle, diddle!
The cat and the fiddle,
The cow jumped over the moon;
The little dog laughed
To see such sport,
And the dish ran away with the spoon.

Mother Goose

Yellow Butter

Yellow butter purple jelly red jam black bread

Spread it thick
Say it quick

Yellow butter purple jelly red jam black bread

Spread it thicker
Say it quicker

Yellow butter purple jelly red jam black bread

Now repeat it
While you eat it

Yellow butter purple jelly red jam black bread

Don't talk
With your mouth full!

Mary Ann Hoberman

The Little Turtle

There was a little turtle,
(Make small circle with hands.)
He lived in a box,
(Make box with both hands.)
He swam in a puddle,
(Wiggle fingers.)
He climbed on the rocks.
(Climb fingers of one hand over the other.)
He snapped at a mosquito,
(Clap hands.)
He snapped at a flea,
(Clap hands.)
He snapped at a minnow,
(Clap hands.)
He snapped at me.
(Point to self.)
He caught the mosquito,
*(Hold hands up, palms facing;
quickly bend fingers shut.)*
He caught the flea,
(Repeat.)
He caught the minnow,
(Repeat.)
But he didn't catch me.
*(Bend fingers only halfway shut and
shake head.)*

Vachel Lindsay

BLAME

I wrote such a beautiful book for you
'Bout rainbows and sunshine
And dreams that come true.
But the goat went and ate it
(You knew that he would),
So I wrote you another one
Fast as I could.
Of course it could never be
Nearly as great
As that beautiful book
That the silly goat ate.
So if you don't like
This new book I just wrote—
Blame the goat.

Shel Silverstein

BEAR IN THERE

There's a Polar Bear
In our Frigidaire—
He likes it 'cause it's cold in there.
With his seat in the meat
And his face in the fish
And his big hairy paws
In the buttery dish,
He's nibbling the noodles,
He's munching the rice,
He's slurping the soda,
He's licking the ice.
And he lets out a roar
If you open the door.
And it gives me a scare
To know he's in there—
That Polary Bear
In our Fridgitydaire.

Shel Silverstein

Five Little Monkeys

Five little monkeys jumping on the bed,
One fell off and broke his head,
Mama called the doctor
And the doctor said,
"No more monkeys jumping on the bed!"

Four little monkeys jumping on the bed,
One fell off and broke his head,
Mama called the doctor
And the doctor said,
"No more monkeys jumping on the bed!"

Three little monkeys jumping on the bed,
One fell off and broke his head,
Mama called the doctor
And the doctor said,
"No more monkeys jumping on the bed!"

Two little monkeys jumping on the bed,
One fell off and broke his head,
Mama called the doctor
And the doctor said,
"No more monkeys jumping on the bed!"

One little monkey jumping on the bed,
One fell off and broke his head,
Mama called the doctor
And the doctor said,
"No more monkeys jumping on the bed!"

What Did You Put in Your Pocket?

What did you put in your pocket
What did you put in your pocket
   in your pockety pockety pocket
Early Monday morning?

I put in some chocolate pudding
I put in some chocolate pudding
   slushy glushy pudding
Early Monday morning.

SLUSHY GLUSHY PUDDING!

What did you put in your pocket
What did you put in your pocket
   in your pockety pockety pocket
Early Tuesday morning?

I put in some ice-cold water
I put in some ice-cold water
   nicy icy water
Early Tuesday morning.

SLUSHY GLUSHY PUDDING!
NICY ICY WATER!

What did you put in your pocket
What did you put in your pocket
   in your pockety pockety pocket
Early Wednesday morning?

I put in a scoop of ice cream
I put in a scoop of ice cream
   slurpy glurpy ice cream
Early Wednesday morning.

SLUSHY GLUSHY PUDDING!
NICY ICY WATER!
SLURPY GLURPY ICE CREAM!

What did you put in your pocket
What did you put in your pocket
   in your pockety pockety pocket
Early Thursday morning?

I put in some mashed potatoes
I put in some mashed potatoes
   fluppy gluppy potatoes
Early Thursday morning.

SLUSHY GLUSHY PUDDING!
NICY ICY WATER!
SLURPY GLURPY ICE CREAM!
FLUPPY GLUPPY POTATOES!

What did you put in your pocket
What did you put in your pocket
   in your pockety pockety pocket
Early Friday morning?

I put in some sticky molasses
I put in some sticky molasses
   sticky icky molasses
Early Friday morning.

SLUSHY GLUSHY PUDDING!
NICY ICY WATER!
SLURPY GLURPY ICE CREAM!
FLUPPY GLUPPY POTATOES!
STICKY ICKY MOLASSES!

What did you put in your pocket
What did you put in your pocket
   in your pockety pockety pocket
Early Saturday morning?

I put in my five fingers
I put in my five fingers
   funny finny fingers
Early Saturday morning.

SLUSHY GLUSHY PUDDING!
NICY ICY WATER!
SLURPY GLURPY ICE CREAM!
FLUPPY GLUPPY POTATOES!
STICKY ICKY MOLASSES!
FUNNY FINNY FINGERS!

What did you put in your pocket
What did you put in your pocket
    in your pockety pockety pocket
Early Sunday morning?

I put in a clean white handkerchief
I put in a clean white handkerchief
    a spinky spanky handkerchief
Early Sunday morning.

SLUSHY GLUSHY PUDDING!
NICY ICY WATER!
SLURPY GLURPY ICE CREAM!
FLUPPY GLUPPY POTATOES!
STICKY ICKY MOLASSES!
FUNNY FINNY FINGERS!
SPINKY SPANKY HANDKERCHIEF!

Beatrice Schenk de Regniers

GOING ON A BEAR HUNT

REFRAIN:
TEACHER: We're going on a Bear Hunt.
CHILDREN: *We're going on a Bear Hunt.*
TEACHER: All righty?
CHILDREN: *All righty.*
TEACHER: Let's go!
CHILDREN: *Let's go!*
(Pattern continues throughout.)

Oh, look!
What's that?
It's a bridge.
We can't go around it.
We can't go under it.
We have to go over it.
All righty?
Let's go!
(Make a thumping noise on chests with fists.)
(Refrain)

Oh, look!
What's that?
It's some grass.
We can't go around it.
We can't go under it.
We have to go through it.
All righty?
Let's go!
(Make swooshing sounds with hands.)
(Refrain)

Oh, look!
What's that?
It's some mud.
We can't go around it.
We can't go under it.
We have to go through it.
All righty?
Let's go!
(Make mushing sounds with hands.)
(Refrain)

Oh, look!
What's that?
It's a tree!
We can't go under it.
We can't go over it.
We have to climb up it!
All righty?
Let's go!
(Make climbing motions and sounds.)
(Refrain)

    Oh, LOOK!!!!!
    WHAT'S THAT?????
    IT'S A BEAR!!
    LET'S GO!!

Down the tree! *(climbing motions)*
Through the mud! *(mud sounds and motions)*
Through the grass! *(grass sounds and motions)*
Over the bridge! *(bridge sounds)*
Run home! *(motions with arms)*
Slam the door! *(door closing motion with a clap sound)*
Whew, we made it! *(wiping brow)*
We weren't afraid,
Were we?
No, not us!

Sing a Song of People

Sing a song of people
   Walking fast or slow;
People in the city,
   Up and down they go.

People on the sidewalk,
People on the bus;
People passing, passing,
In back and front of us.
People on the subway
Underneath the ground;
People riding taxis
Round and round and round.

People with their hats on,
Going in the doors;
People with umbrellas
When it rains and pours.
People in tall buildings
And in stores below;
Riding elevators
Up and down they go.
People walking singly,
People in a crowd;

People saying nothing,
People talking loud.
People laughing, smiling,
Grumpy people too;
People who just hurry
And never look at you!

Sing a song of people
   Who like to come and go;
Sing of city people
   You see but never know!

Lois Lenski

Mr. Backward

Mr. Backward lives in town.
He never wakes up, he always wakes down.
He eats dessert before his meal.
His plastic plants and flowers are real.
He takes a bath inside his sink
And cleans his clothes with purple ink.
He wears his earmuffs on his nose
And a woolen scarf around his toes.
He loves his gloves worn inside out.
He combs his hair with sauerkraut.
His black dog, Spot, is colored green.
His grandmama is seventeen.
He rakes the leaves still on the trees
And bakes a cake with antifreeze.
He goes to sleep beneath his bed
While wearing slippers on his head.

Douglas Florian

Little Seeds

Little seeds we sow in spring,
Growing while the robins sing,
Give us carrots, peas and beans,
Tomatoes, pumpkins, squash
and greens.

And we pick them,
One and all,
Through the summer,
Through the fall.

Winter comes, then spring, and then
Little seeds we sow again.

Else Holmelund Minarik

Tommy

I put a seed into the ground
And said, "I'll watch it grow."
I watered it and cared for it
As well as I could know.

One day I walked in my back yard,
And oh, what did I see!
My seed had popped itself right out,
Without consulting me.

Gwendolyn Brooks

My Pet Spider

Last week my pet spider was so lonely that she crawled out of her cage to look for some friends.

On Monday she . . .
      went to the lake to look for the snake,
      but no one was home so she went back alone.

On Tuesday she . . .
      went to the log to look for the frog;
      went to the lake to look for the snake;
      but no one was home so she went back alone.

On Wednesday she . . .
      went to the thicket to look for the cricket;
      went to the log to look for the frog;
      went to the lake to look for the snake;
      but no one was home so she went back alone.

On Thursday she . . .

    went to the tree to look for the flea;
    went to the thicket to look for the cricket;
    went to the log to look for the frog;
    went to the lake to look for the snake;
    but no one was home so she went back alone.

On Friday she . . .

    went to the hole to look for the mole;
    went to the tree to look for the flea;
    went to the thicket to look for the cricket;
    went to the log to look for the frog;
    went to the lake to look for the snake;
    but no one was home so she went back alone.

On Saturday she . . .
      went to the plant to look for the ant;
      went to the hole to look for the mole;
      went to the tree to look for the flea;
      went to the thicket to look for the cricket;
      went to the log to look for the frog;
      went to the lake to look for the snake;
      but no one was home so she went back alone.

On Sunday she decided to look once more for some friends,
so she . . .
      went to the plant and found the ant;
      went to the hole and found the mole;
      went to the tree and found the flea;
      went to the thicket and found the cricket;
      went to the log and found the frog;
      went to the lake and found the snake;

Then she went back home no longer alone!

Jane Simon

When All the World's Asleep

Where do insects go at night,
When all the world's asleep?
Where do bugs and butterflies
And caterpillars creep?

Turtles sleep inside their shells;
The robin has her nest.
Rabbits and the sly old fox
Have holes where they can rest.

Bears can crawl inside a cave;
The lion has his den.
Cows can sleep inside the barn,
And pigs can use their pen.

But where do bugs and butterflies
And caterpillars creep,
When everything is dark outside
And all the world's asleep?

Anita E. Posey

Fireflies, Fireflies

Fireflies, fireflies,
Tiny lanterns in the sky,
You fly up high,
You fly down low;
Now on sister's
Dress you glow.

adapted by Demi

Little Silk Worms

Little silk worms, if you please,
Eat up all the mulberry leaves.
Make cocoons as white as milk,
And we'll make clothes of purest silk.

adapted by Demi

IF YOU EVER

If you ever ever ever ever ever
If you ever ever ever meet a whale
You must never never never never never
You must never never never touch its tail:
For if you ever ever ever ever ever,
If you ever ever ever touch its tail,
You will never never never never never,
You will never never meet another whale.

Charlotte Pomerantz

THE FISH WITH THE DEEP SEA SMILE

They fished and they fished
Way down in the sea,
Down in the sea a mile,
They fished among all the fish in the sea
For the fish with the deep sea smile.

One fish came up from the deep of the sea,
From down in the sea a mile,
It had blue green eyes
And whiskers three
But never a deep sea smile.

One fish came up from the deep of the sea,
From down in the sea a mile,
With electric lights up and down his tail
But never a deep sea smile.

They fished and they fished
Way down in the sea,
Down in the sea a mile,
They fished among all the fish in the sea
For the fish with the deep sea smile.

One fish came up with terrible teeth,
One fish with long strong jaws,
One fish came up with long stalked eyes,
One fish with terrible claws.

They fished all through the ocean deep
For many and many a mile,
And they caught a fish with a laughing eye
But none with a deep sea smile.

And then one day they got a pull
From down in the sea a mile,
And when they pulled the fish into the boat
He smiled a deep sea smile.

And as he smiled, the hook got free
And then, what a deep sea smile!
He flipped his tail and swam away
Down in the sea a mile.

Margaret Wise Brown

I'll tell you a Story

I'll tell you a story
About Jack-a-Nory:
And now my story's begun.
I'll tell you another
About his big brother:
And now my story is done.

The Hare and the Tortoise

an Aesop Fable
retold by
Stephanie Calmenson

One day, Hare was bragging loudly to the circle of animals who had gathered round him. "Not only am I handsome," said Hare, "but I am fast! No one is faster than I!"

At that moment, Tortoise came along and broke into the circle. "You may be fast, Hare," said Tortoise quietly, "but I would like to race you. I am sure that I will win."

Hare threw back his head and laughed. "Why, you are the slowest thing on four feet, Tortoise. How could you possibly win a race with me?"

"Will you let me try?" Tortoise asked.

Hare agreed to the race. The other animals set the course to be run and made a starting line.

Fox was chosen to start the race. "On your mark. Get set. Go!" she said.

Hare took off at top speed, leaving Tortoise in the dust. He looked back to see Tortoise growing smaller and smaller in the distance. When he could see no sign of Tortoise at all, Hare stopped running.

"What a silly creature Tortoise is, to think that he could win this race. It was nice of me to agree to it, but there's no need to tire myself out. I think I'll just stop here for a little nap."

With that, Hare went off the road to a grassy spot, leaned back against a rock and closed his eyes.

Meantime, Tortoise plodded on at his own steady pace. Hare was nowhere in sight, but Tortoise was not worried. "I'll just do my best," thought Tortoise. It wasn't long before he passed Hare.

When Hare woke up from his nap, he yawned and stretched.

"Now, what am I doing here?" he wondered aloud. "Ah, yes, I am racing. Racing with Tortoise." He chuckled at the thought, then continued down the road toward the finish line.

Hare looked behind him, but saw no sign of Tortoise. This time he should have been looking ahead. For as soon as he turned the bend he found Tortoise, on the winning side of the finish line, resting in the shade of a big oak tree.

SLOW BUT STEADY
WINS THE RACE.

LET'S GO, FROGGY!

by Jonathan London • illustrated by Frank Remkiewicz

It was warm.
Froggy woke up
and looked out the window.
Birds, butterflies, flowers.
"Hurray!" sang Froggy.
"I want to go out and play!"

"Okay," said his father.
"How about a bike trip
and a picnic?
Would you like that?"

"Yes!" cried Froggy. "Let's go!"

"First you have to get ready, silly,"
said his father.
"Okay!" said Froggy. "I'm getting
ready!"

So Froggy got dressed.
He pulled on his underwear—*zap!*
Pulled on his shorts—*zip!*

Pulled on his socks—*zoop!*
Pulled on his sneakers—*zup!*
and buttoned up his shirt—*zut!*
zut! zut!

FRRROOGGYY!

called his father. "Let's go!"
"I'm re-e-a-d-y!" yelled Froggy
and flopped out to show him—
flop flop flop.

"But Froggy!" said his father.
"You need your bicycle helmet!"
"I don't know where it is!" said
Froggy.
"It's wherever you left it!"
"I forget!"
"You have to *look* for it!"

So Froggy looked for his helmet.
He looked under the sink—
bonk!
He looked under the fridge—
slam!

He looked in his
toy chest.
"I found it!"
yelled Froggy
and put it
on with a
slap—*zat!*

FRRROOGGYY!
called his father.
"Let's go!"
"I'm re-e-a-d-y!" yelled
Froggy—*flop flop flop.*

"You should bring your
butterfly net!" said his father.
"I don't know where it is!"
"It's wherever you left it!"

So Froggy looked for
his butterfly net.
He looked under the coffee
table—*bonk!*
He looked in the garbage
can—*slam!*

He looked in his father's
golf bag.
"I found it!" yelled Froggy
and swung it at a fly—*swish!*—
but missed.

FRRROOGGYY!
called his father. "Let's go!"
"I'm re-e-a-d-y!" yelled
Froggy—*flop flop flop.*

"How about the ball that
Grandpapa gave you?" asked
his father.
"I don't know where it is!"
"It's wherever you left it!"

So Froggy looked for his ball.
He looked under the stove—
bonk!
He looked in the cookie jar—
slam!

He looked in the bathtub.
"I found it!" he yelled and
kicked it into the goldfish
bowl—*splash!*

FRRROOGGYY!
called his father. "Let's go!"
"I'm re-e-a-d-y!" yelled
Froggy—*flop flop flop.*

"Let's bring the bag of peaches
Auntie Loulou gave you," said
his father.
"I don't know where it is!"
"It's wherever you left it!"

So Froggy looked for the bag of
peaches.
He looked under the kitchen
table—*bonk!*
He looked in his closet—*slam!*

He looked in his bed.
"I found it!" yelled Froggy
and took a bite—*scrunch!*
(He was getting kind of
hungry.)

FRRROOGGYY!
called his father. "Let's go!"
"I'm re-e-a-d-y!"
yelled Froggy—
flop flop flop.

"Daddy, can I bring the pack of trading cards Uncle Gerard gave me?"
"Okay, Froggy, but hurry. Let's go!"
"I don't know where it is!"
"It's wherever you left it!"

"*Oops!* Here it is! I found it!
It was in my pocket!
Can we go now, Daddy? I'm *ready!*"

"Okay, but do you know where my red backpack is?" asked his father.

"Daddy! *It's wherever you left it!*"

"I forget!"

Froggy pointed.

IT'S ON YOUR BACK!

Froggy laughed.
"*Oops!*" cried Froggy's father,
looking more red in the face than green.

Ready to go at last, Froggy flopped
over to the bicycle—*flop flop flop.*

"Let's go, Froggy!" said his father.
"I'm hungry!" said Froggy. "I want to eat NOW!"

So they ate their picnic
on the patio—*munch scrunch munch.*

"Okay, I'm ready!" said Froggy.
"Let's go!" said his father.

And off they pedaled into the
sunset—*wee!*

The GINGERBREAD MAN

retold by Anne Rockwell

Once upon a time there was a little old woman and a little old man, and they lived all alone. They were very happy together, but they wanted a child and since they had none, they decided to make one out of gingerbread. So one day the little old woman and the little old man made themselves a little gingerbread man, and they put him in the oven to bake.

When the gingerbread man was done, the little old woman opened the oven door and pulled out the pan. Out jumped the little gingerbread man—and away he ran. The little old woman and the little old man ran after him as fast as they could, but he just laughed and said,

"Run, run, as fast as you can.
You can't catch me!
I'm the Gingerbread Man!"

And they couldn't catch him.

The gingerbread man ran on and on until he came to a cow. "Stop, little gingerbread man," said the cow. "I want to eat you."

But the gingerbread man said, "I have run away from a little old woman and a little old man, and I can run away from you, too. I can, I can!"

And the cow began to chase the gingerbread man, but the gingerbread man ran faster and said,

"Run, run, as fast as you can.
You can't catch me!
I'm the Gingerbread Man!"

And the cow couldn't catch him.

The gingerbread man ran on until he came to a horse. "Please, stop, little gingerbread man," said the horse. "I want to eat you."

And the gingerbread man said, "I have run away from a little old woman, a little old man, and a cow, and I can run away from you, too. I can, I can!"

And the horse began to chase the gingerbread man, but the gingerbread man ran faster and called to the horse,

"Run, run, as fast as you can.
You can't catch me!
I'm the Gingerbread Man!"

And the horse couldn't catch him.

By and by the gingerbread man came to a field full of farmers. "Stop," said the farmers. "Don't run so fast. We want to eat you." But the gingerbread man said, "I have run away from a little old woman, a little old man, a cow, and a horse, and I can run away from you, too. I can, I can!" And the farmers began to chase him, but the gingerbread man ran faster than ever and said,

"Run, run, as fast as you can.
You can't catch me!
I'm the Gingerbread Man!"

And the farmers couldn't catch him.

The gingerbread man ran faster and faster. He ran past a school full of children.

"Stop, little gingerbread man," said the children. "We want to eat you."

But the gingerbread man said, "I have run away from a little old woman, a little old man, a cow, a horse, and a field full of farmers, and I can run away from you, too. I can, I can!"

And the children began to chase him, but the gingerbread man ran faster as he said,

"Run, run, as fast as you can.
You can't catch me!
I'm the Gingerbread Man!"

And the children couldn't catch him.

By this time the gingerbread man was so proud of himself, he didn't think anyone could catch him. Pretty soon he saw a fox. The fox looked at him and began to run after him.

But the gingerbread man said, "You can't catch me! I have run away from a little old woman, a little old man, a cow, a horse, a field full of farmers, and a school full of children, and I can run away from you, too. I can, I can!

"Run, run, as fast as you can.
You can't catch me!
I'm the Gingerbread Man!"

"Oh," said the fox, "I do not want to catch you. I only want to help you run away."

Just then the gingerbread man came to a river. He could not swim across, and he had to keep running.

"Jump on my tail," said the fox. "I will take you across."

So the gingerbread man jumped on the fox's tail, and the fox began to swim across the river. When he had gone a little way, he said to the gingerbread man, "You are too heavy on my tail. Jump on my back."

And the gingerbread man did.

The fox swam a little farther, and then he said, "I am afraid you will get wet on my back. Jump on my shoulder." And the gingerbread man did.

In the middle of the river, the fox said, "Oh, dear, my shoulder is sinking. Jump on my nose, and I can hold you out of the water."

So the little gingerbread man jumped on the fox's nose, and the fox threw back his head and snapped his sharp teeth.

"Oh, dear," said the gingerbread man, "I am a quarter gone!"

The next minute he said, "Now I am half gone!"

And the next minute he said, "Oh, my goodness gracious! I am three quarters gone!"

And then the gingerbread man never said anything more at all.

STONE SOUP

retold by Ann McGovern

A young man was walking. He walked and he walked. He walked all night. And he walked all day. He was tired. And he was hungry.

At last he came to a big house. "What a fine house," he said. "There will be plenty of food for me here."

He knocked on the door. A little old lady opened it. "Good lady," said the young man, "I am very hungry. Can you give me something to eat?"

"I have nothing to give you," said the little old lady. "I have nothing in the house. I have nothing in the garden." And she began to close the door.

"Stop," said the young man. "If you will not give me something to eat, will you give me a stone?"

"A stone?" said the little old lady. "What will you do with a stone? You cannot eat a stone!"

"Ah," said the young man. "I can make soup from a stone."

Now the little old lady had never heard of that. Make soup from a stone? Fancy that. "There are stones in the road," said the little old lady.

The young man picked up a round, gray stone. "This stone will make wonderful soup," he said. "Now get me a pot."

The little old lady got a pot.

"Fill the pot with water and put it on the fire," the young man said.

The little old lady did as she was told. And soon the water was bubbling in the pot. The young man put the round, gray stone into the pot. "Now we will wait for the stone to cook into soup," he said.

The pot bubbled and bubbled. After a while, the little old lady said, "This soup is cooking fast."

"It is cooking fast now," said the hungry young man. "But it would cook faster with some onions." So the little old lady went to the garden to get some yellow onions.

Into the pot went the yellow onions, with the round, gray stone. "Soup from a stone," said the little old lady. "Fancy that."

The pot bubbled and bubbled. After a while, the little old lady said, "This soup smells good."

"It smells good now," said the hungry young man. "But it would smell better with some carrots." So the little old lady went out to the garden and pulled up all the carrots she could carry.

Into the pot went the long, thin carrots, with the yellow onions, and the round, gray stone. "Soup from a stone," said the little old lady. "Fancy that."

The pot bubbled and bubbled. After a while, the little old lady said, "This soup tastes good."

"It tastes good now," said the hungry young man. "But it would taste better with beef bones." So the little old lady went to get some juicy beef bones.

Into the pot went the juicy beef bones, with the long, thin carrots, and the yellow onions, and the round, gray stone. "Soup from a stone," said the little old lady. "Fancy that."

The pot bubbled and bubbled. After a while, the little old lady said, "This soup is fit for a prince."

"It is fit for a prince now," said the hungry young man. "But it would be fit for a king with a bit of pepper and a handful of salt." So the little old lady got the pepper and the salt.

Into the pot went the bit of pepper and the handful of salt, with the juicy beef bones, and the long, thin carrots, and the yellow onions, and the round, gray stone. "Soup from a stone," said the little old lady. "Fancy that."

The pot bubbled and bubbled. After a while, the little old lady said, "This soup is too thin."

"It is too thin now," said the hungry young man. "But it would be nice and thick with some butter and barley." So the little old lady went to get butter and barley.

Into the pot went the butter and barley, with the bit of pepper and the handful of salt, and the juicy beef bones, and the long, thin carrots, and the yellow onions, and the round, gray stone.

"Soup from a stone," said the little old lady. "Fancy that."

The pot bubbled and bubbled. After a while, the little old lady tasted the soup again. "That is good soup," she said.

"Yes," said the hungry young man. "This soup is fit for a king. Now we will eat it."

"Stop!" said the little old lady. "This soup is indeed fit for a king. Now I will set a table fit for a king." So she took out her best tablecloth and her best dishes.

Then the little old lady and the hungry young man ate all the soup—
the soup made with
the butter and barley,
and the bit of pepper
and the handful of salt,
and the juicy beef bones,
and the long, thin carrots,
and the yellow onions,
and the round, gray stone.

"Soup from a stone," said the little old lady. "Fancy that."

"Now I must be on my way," said the young man. He took the stone out of the pot, and put it into his pocket.

"Why are you taking the stone?" said the little old lady.

"Well," said the young man. "The stone is not cooked enough. I will have to cook it some more tomorrow." And the young man said good-bye. He walked on down the road. He walked and he walked. "What a fine supper I will have tomorrow," he said to himself. "Soup from a stone. Fancy that."

THE
LION AND
THE MOUSE

an Aesop fable retold by Anne Rockwell

A lion lay sleeping. A little mouse ran across his paw. That tickled the lion and woke him up. He roared and grabbed the little mouse.

"Please," said the little mouse, "do not hurt me. I am sorry I woke you up, but if you do not hurt me, I promise I will do something good for you someday."

The lion laughed. "How silly," he thought. "What could a tiny little mouse do for a big, strong lion like me?" But he let him go.

Soon after, the lion was walking through the forest when suddenly he was caught in a net some hunters had made to trap him. He roared and roared, and his roars made the leaves on the trees tremble, but still he could not free himself from the net.

Far away the little mouse heard him roar. He hurried to the place where the big lion lay trapped.

"Remember, I promised you I would someday do something good for you," said the little mouse, and he began to nibble on the ropes of the net with his sharp little teeth. He nibbled and nibbled and nibbled some more until there was a big hole in the net.

Then the lion was free, and the lion and the mouse walked away together.

The Three Billy-Goats Gruff

retold by P. C. Asbjörnsen

Once upon a time there were three billy-goats, who wanted to go up to the hillside to make themselves fat, and the name of all three was Gruff.

On the way up was a bridge over a mountain stream they had to cross; and under the bridge lived a great ugly Troll, with eyes as big as saucers, and a nose as long as a poker.

The first to cross the bridge was the youngest billy-goat Gruff.

"Trip, trap! Trip, trap!" went the bridge.

"Who's that tripping over my bridge?" roared the Troll.

"Oh! It is only I, the tiniest billy-goat Gruff; and I'm going up to the hillside to make myself fat," said the billy-goat with such a small voice.

"Well, I'm coming to gobble you up," said the Troll.

"Oh, no! Please don't gobble me up. I'm too little, that I am," said the billy-goat. "Wait a bit till the second billy-goat Gruff comes. He's much bigger."

"Well! Be off with you," said the Troll.

A little while later the second billy-goat Gruff came to cross the bridge.

"Trip, trap! Trip, trap! Trip, trap!" went the bridge.

"Who's that tripping over my bridge?" roared the Troll.

"Oh! It's I, the second billy-goat Gruff, and I'm going up to the hillside to make myself fat," said the billy-goat, who hadn't such a small voice.

"Well, I'm coming to gobble you up," said the Troll.

"Oh, no! Please don't gobble me up. Wait a little till the big billy-goat Gruff comes. He's much bigger."

"Very well! Be off with you," said the Troll.

But just then up came the big billy-goat Gruff.

"*Trip, trap! Trip, trap! Trip, trap!*" went the bridge, for the billy-goat was so heavy that the bridge creaked and groaned under him.

"*Who's that* tramping over my bridge?" roared the Troll.

"*It's I! The big billy-goat Gruff,*" said the billy-goat, who had an ugly, hoarse voice of his own.

"Well, I'm coming to gobble you up," roared the Troll.

> "*Well, come along!*
> *I've got two spears,*
> *And I'll poke your nose*
> *and pierce your ears;*
> *I've got besides two curling stones,*
> *And I'll bruise your body*
> *and rattle your bones.*"

That was what the big billy-goat said; and then he flew at the Troll and tossed him into the water. And the third billy-goat Gruff went up to the hillside. There the billy-goats got so fat they were scarcely able to walk home again; and if the fat hasn't fallen off them, why they're still fat, and so:

> *Snip, snap, snout,*
> *This tale's told out.*

Chicken Forgets

by Miska Miles

"Chicken," the mother hen said, "I need your help. I want you to go berry hunting. I need a basket of wild blackberries."

"I'd like to go berry hunting," the little chicken said.

"Take this basket and fill it to the top," the mother hen said. "Sometimes you forget things. This time, please, please keep your mind on what you are doing. Don't forget."

"I won't forget," the little chicken said. "I'll hunt for wild blackberries."

He started across the meadow. And because he didn't want to forget, he said to himself over and over again, "Get wild black-berries. Get wild blackberries."

All the way to the narrow river he kept saying, "Get wild blackberries."

Then the chicken heard the rusty voice of an old frog.

"What are you saying?" the frog asked.

"Get wild blackberries," the chicken said.

"If you're talking to me, you shouldn't say that," the frog said.

"Oh?" said the chicken. "What should I say?"

"Get a big green fly," the frog said.

The chicken went on his way. And because he didn't want to forget, he said to himself, "Get a big green fly. Get a big green fly."

All the way to the pasture he said, "Get a big green fly."

At the pasture, a goat pushed his head through the rails of the fence and twitched his beard.

"If you are talking to ME," he

said, "you should NOT say 'Get a green fly.' You should say, 'Get green weeds.'"

"Oh?" said the chicken. And on he went, past the pasture, saying, "Get green weeds. Get green weeds."

A bee buzzed over his head.

"What are you mumbling?" the bee asked.

"I was only saying 'Get weeds,'" the chicken said.

"I think that's wrong," the bee said. "You should say, 'Get clover blossoms.'"

So the little chicken said, "Get clover blossoms."

He said, "Get clover blossoms" all the way to the edge of the cornfield.

"No, no," said a robin. "Berries are better. Follow me."

So the little chicken ran along the ground, following the robin's shadow, and he came to a beautiful patch of wild blackberries. The robin flew down and ate until he could eat no more.

And the little chicken filled his basket with beautiful, shining wild blackberries. He started home.

Back he went, through the cornfield and beside the pasture fence by the river.

He ate five berries.

Across the meadow he went.

And he ate three berries.

At home, the mother hen looked at the basket.

"You DIDN'T forget," she said. "You brought home blackberries, and the basket is almost full."

The little chicken said, "It's easy to remember when you really try."

"I'm proud of you," his mother said.

And the little chicken was proud, too.

Franklin in the Dark

by Paulette Bourgeois

illustrated by Brenda Clark

Franklin could slide down a riverbank all by himself. He could count forwards and backwards. He could even zip zippers and button buttons. But Franklin was afraid of small, dark places and that was a problem because Franklin was a turtle. He was afraid of crawling into his small, dark shell. And so, Franklin the turtle dragged his shell behind him.

Every night, Franklin's mother would take a flashlight and shine it into his shell.

"See," she would say, "there's nothing to be afraid of."

She always said that. She wasn't afraid of anything. But Franklin was sure that creepy things, slippery things, and monsters lived inside his small, dark shell.

So Franklin went looking for help. He walked until he met a duck.

"Excuse me, Duck. I'm afraid of small, dark places and I can't crawl inside my shell. Can you help me?"

"Maybe," quacked the duck. "You see, I'm afraid of very deep water. Sometimes, when nobody is watching, I wear water wings. Would my water wings help you?"

"No," said Franklin. "I'm not afraid of water."

So Franklin walked and walked and walked until he met a lion.

"Excuse me, Lion. I'm afraid of small, dark places and I can't crawl inside my shell. Can you help me?"

"Maybe," roared the lion. "You see, I'm afraid of great, loud noises. Sometimes, when nobody is looking, I wear ear-muffs. Would my earmuffs help you?"

"No," said Franklin. "I'm not afraid of great, loud noises."

So Franklin walked and walked and walked until he met a bird.

"Excuse me, Bird. I'm afraid of small, dark places and I can't crawl inside my shell. Can you help me?"

"Maybe," chirped the bird. "I'm afraid of flying so high that I get dizzy and fall to the ground. Sometimes, when nobody is looking, I pull my parachute. Would my parachute help you?"

"No," said Franklin. "I'm not afraid of flying high and getting dizzy."

So Franklin walked and walked and walked until he met a polar bear.

"Excuse me, Polar Bear. I'm afraid of small, dark places and I can't crawl inside my shell. Can you help me?"

"Maybe," growled the bear. "You see, I'm afraid of freezing on icy, cold nights. Sometimes, when nobody is looking, I wear my snowsuit to bed. Would my snowsuit help you?"

"No," said Franklin. "I'm not afraid of freezing on icy, cold nights."

Franklin was tired and hungry. He walked and walked and walked until he met his mother.

"Oh, Franklin. I was so afraid you were lost."

"You were afraid? I didn't know mothers were ever afraid," said Franklin.

"Well, did you find some help?" she asked.

"No. I met a duck who was afraid of deep water."

"Hmmm," she said.

"Then I met a lion who was afraid of great, loud noises."

"Uh, hmmm," she said.

"And then I met a bird who was afraid of falling and a polar bear who was afraid of freezing."

"Oh," she said, "they were all afraid of something."

"Hmmmm," said Franklin.

It was getting late. Franklin was very tired and very hungry. They walked and walked until they were home.

Franklin's mother gave him a cold supper and a warm hug. And then she sent him off to bed.

"Goodnight, dear," she said.

Well, Franklin knew what he had to do. He crawled right inside his small, dark shell. He was sure he saw creepy things, slippery things, and a monster. But he said a brave "Goodnight."

And then, when nobody was looking, Franklin the turtle turned on his night light.

Mother, Mother, I Want Another

by Maria Polushkin

illustrated by Diane Dawson

It was bedtime in the mouse house. Mrs. Mouse took baby mouse to his room. She helped him put on his pajamas and told him to brush his teeth. She tucked him into his bed and read him a bedtime story. She gave him a bedtime kiss, and then she said "Goodnight." But as she was leaving, baby mouse started to cry. "Why are you crying?" asked Mrs. Mouse.

"I want another, Mother."

"Another mother!" cried Mrs. Mouse. "Where will I find another mother for my baby?"

Mrs. Mouse ran to get Mrs. Duck.

"Please, Mrs. Duck, come to our house and help put baby mouse to bed. Tonight he wants another mother."

Mrs. Duck came and sang a song:

Quack, quack, mousie,
Don't you fret.
I'll bring you worms
Both fat and wet.

But baby mouse said, "Mother, Mother, I want another."

Mrs. Duck went to get Mrs. Frog. Mrs. Frog came and sang:

Croak, croak, mousie,
Close your eyes.
I will bring you
Big fat flies.

But baby mouse said, "Mother, Mother, I want another."

Mrs. Frog went to get Mrs. Pig. Mrs. Pig came and sang a song:

Oink, oink, mousie,
Go to sleep.
I'll bring some carrots
For you to keep.

But baby mouse said, "Mother, Mother, I want another."

Mrs. Pig went to get Mrs. Donkey. Mrs. Donkey came and sang a song:

Hee-haw, mousie,
Hush-a-bye.
I'll sing for you
A lullaby.

But baby mouse had had enough. "NO MORE MOTHERS!" he shouted. "I want another KISS."

"Really?"

"Well, now!"

"Oh?"

"Indeed?"

"I see."

Mrs. Duck kissed baby mouse. Mrs. Frog kissed baby mouse. Mrs. Pig kissed baby mouse. And Mrs. Donkey kissed baby mouse.

Then Mrs. Mouse gave baby mouse a drink of water. She tucked in his blanket. And she gave him a kiss. Baby mouse smiled. "May I have another, Mother?"

"Of course," said Mrs. Mouse, and she leaned over and gave him *another* kiss.

The Three Bears

retold by Anne Rockwell

Once upon a time there were three bears who lived together in a house of their own in the woods. One of them was a little wee bear, and one was a middle-sized bear, and the third was a great big bear. They each had a bowl for their porridge—a little bowl for the little wee bear, and a middle-sized bowl for the middle-sized bear, and a great big bowl for the great big bear. And they each had a chair to sit on—a little chair for the little wee bear, and a middle-sized chair for the middle-sized bear, and a great big chair for the great big bear. And they each had a bed to sleep in—a little bed for the little wee bear, and a middle-sized bed for the middle-sized bear, and a great big bed for the great big bear.

One day, after they had made the porridge for their breakfast and poured it into their bowls, they walked out in the woods while the porridge was cooling. A little girl named Goldilocks passed by the house and looked in at the window. And then she looked in at the keyhole, and when she saw that there was no one home, she lifted the latch on the door.

The door was not locked because the bears were good bears who never did anyone any harm and never thought that anyone would harm them. So Goldilocks opened the door and walked in. She was very glad to see the porridge on the table, as she was hungry from walking in the woods, and so she set about helping herself.

First she tasted the porridge of the great big bear, but that was too hot for her. Next she tasted the porridge of the middle-sized bear, but that was too cold for her. And then she tasted the porridge of the little wee bear, and that was neither too hot nor too cold but just right, and she liked it so much that she ate it all up.

Then Goldilocks sat down on the chair of the great big bear, but that was too hard for her. And then she sat down on the chair of the middle-sized bear, and that was too soft for her. And then she sat down on the chair of the little wee bear, and that was neither too hard nor too soft, but just right. So she seated herself in it, and there she sat until she sat the bottom out of the chair and down she came upon the floor.

Then Goldilocks went upstairs to the bedroom where the three bears slept. And first she lay down upon the bed of the great big bear, but that was too high for her.

And next she lay down upon the bed of the middle-sized bear, but that was too low for her. But when she lay down upon the bed of the little wee bear, it was neither too high nor too low, but just right. So she covered herself up comfortably and fell fast asleep.

When the three bears thought their porridge would be cool enough for them to eat, they came home for breakfast. Now Goldilocks had left the spoon of the great big bear standing in the porridge.

"Somebody has been eating my porridge!" said the great big bear in a great, rough gruff voice.

Then the middle-sized bear looked at its porridge and saw the spoon was standing in it, too.

"Somebody has been eating *my* porridge!" said the middle-sized bear in a middle-sized voice.

Then the little wee bear looked at its bowl, and there was the spoon standing in the bowl, but the porridge was all gone.

"Somebody has been eating my porridge and has eaten it all up!" said the little wee bear in a little wee voice.

Upon this, the three bears, seeing that someone had come into their house and eaten up all the little wee bear's breakfast, began to look around them.

Now Goldilocks had not put the cushion straight when she rose from the chair of the great big bear.

"Somebody has been sitting in my chair!" said the great big bear in a great, rough gruff voice.

And Goldilocks had squashed down the soft cushion of the middle-sized bear.

"Somebody has been sitting in my chair!" said the middle-sized bear in a middle-sized voice.

HONEY

"Somebody has been sitting in my chair, and has sat the bottom through!" said the little wee bear in a little wee voice.

Then the three bears thought that they had better look further in case it was a burglar, so they went upstairs into their bedroom. Now Goldilocks had pulled the pillow of the great big bear out of its place.

"Somebody has been lying in my bed!" said the great big bear in a great, rough gruff voice.

And Goldilocks had pulled the cover of the middle-sized bear out of its place.

"Somebody has been lying in my bed!" said the middle-sized bear in a middle-sized voice.

But when the little wee bear came to look at its bed, there was the pillow in its place. But *upon* the pillow? There was Goldilocks' head, which was not in its place, for she had no business there.

"Somebody has been lying in my bed, and here she is still," said the little wee bear in a little wee voice.

Now Goldilocks had heard in her sleep the great, rough gruff voice of the great big bear, but she was so fast asleep that it was no more to her than the rumbling of distant thunder. And she had heard the middle-sized voice of the middle-sized bear, but it was only as if she had heard someone speaking in a dream. But when she heard the little wee voice of the little wee bear, it was so sharp and so shrill that it woke her up at once.

Up she sat, and when she saw the three bears on one side of the bed, she tumbled out at the other and ran to the window. Now the window was open, for the bears were good, tidy bears who always opened their bedroom window in the morning to let in the fresh air and sunshine. So Goldilocks jumped out through the window and ran away, and the three bears never saw anything more of her.

THE TERRIBLE TRAGADABAS

A New Mexican folktale

retold by Joe Hayes

Long ago there was an old woman with three granddaughters. She called them Little Bitty . . . Middle Size . . . and Great Big. They were good girls and they always helped their grandma with the work around the house.

One day the grandma was mending her granddaughters' socks. She sat in her rocking chair and the girls came and sat on the floor in front of her.

The grandma gave one pair of little socks to Little Bitty. She gave two pairs of middle-size socks to Middle Size. And three pairs of big socks she gave to Great Big.

They all started sewing.

It wasn't very long before Little Bitty looked up and said, "Grandma, I'm all done!"

The grandma smiled. "Oh, what a good girl you are! You can go down to the store and buy some little cakes and honey!"

She gave her some money. The girl went skipping down the street, singing to herself.

She got to the store, but the door was closed. So she knocked— tap-tap-tap.

From inside the store, a voice roared, "WHO IS IT?"

The girl answered, "I'm Little Bitty."

The voice said,

"LITTLE BITTY, LITTLE BITTY,
DON'T YOU COME INSIDE.
I'M THE TRAGADABAS,
AND I'LL SWALLOW YOU ALIVE!"

But Little Bitty had never heard about the Terrible Tragadabas. She said, "Tragadabas? What's a Tragadabas?"

She opened the door—creeaaaak.

She went inside and looked around.

She didn't see anyone.

But suddenly . . . out jumped . . .

THE TRAGADABAS!

The girl ran out the door and up the street as fast as her little bitty legs could carry her. She came to a big green tree and

shinnied up to a high branch.

And she didn't come down again!

Back at home the grandma was rocking and stitching, rocking and stitching. Then, Middle Size looked up and said, "Grandma, I'm all done!"

The grandma said, "What a good girl you are! You can go down to the store and buy some little cakes and honey."

Middle Size went skipping down the street, singing to herself.

She got to the store, but the door was closed. So she knocked—Tap-Tap-Tap.

"WHO IS IT?"

"I'm Middle Size."

"MIDDLE SIZE, MIDDLE SIZE,
DON'T YOU COME INSIDE.
I'M THE TRAGADABAS,
AND I'LL SWALLOW YOU ALIVE!"

But Middle Size shrugged, "Tragadabas? What's a Tragadabas?"

She opened the door—creeaaaak.

She went inside . . .

Out jumped . . .

THE TRAGADABAS!

The girl ran out the door and up the street as fast as her middle size legs could carry her. She came to the big green tree and she shinnied up to an even higher branch.

And she didn't come down again!

At home the grandma was rocking and stitching, rocking and stitching. Great Big looked up and said, "Grandma, I'm all done!"

"What a good girl you are! You can go down to the store and buy some little cakes and honey!"

Great Big went skipping down the street, singing to herself. She got to the store. The door was closed. She knocked—TAP-TAP-TAP.

"WHO IS IT?"
"I'm Great Big!"
　　"GREAT BIG, GREAT BIG,
　　DON'T YOU COME INSIDE.
　　I'M THE TRAGADABAS,
　　AND I'LL SWALLOW YOU ALIVE!"
"Tragadabas? What's a Tragadabas?"
She opened the door—creeaaaak . . .
Out jumped . . .
THE TRAGADABAS!
She ran out the door and up the street as fast as her great big legs could carry her! She came to the big green tree and shinnied up to the highest branch of all.

She didn't come down again!

At home the grandma was rocking and stitching, rocking and stitching. She said, "Where are those girls? I'll have to go and get them!"

She took her walking stick and she tottered down to the store. With her stick she knocked on the door—tap-tap-tap-tap.

"WHO IS IT?"
"I'm the grandma."
　　"GRANDMA, GRANDMA,
　　DON'T YOU COME INSIDE.
　　I'M THE TRAGADABAS,
　　AND I'LL SWALLOW YOU ALIVE!"
The grandma knew all about the Terrible Tragadabas. She gasped, "The Tragadabas! He must have swallowed my grandchildren!"

She walked away crying to herself.

But just then—bzzzzzzzzz—a great big bumblebee came flying down the street. The bee said, "Bzzzzzzz . . . Grandma, why are you crying?"

The grandma sobbed, "It's because the Tragadabas has swallowed my grandchildren."

The bee said, "Bzzzzz . . . I'm not afraid of the Tragadabas."

The bee buzzed down the street and up to the store. With her little foot she knocked—tip-tip-tip.

"WHO IS IT?"

The bee answered,

"I am the bumblebee
with a stinger on my rump.
And when I start to sting you,
I'll really make you jump."

And the bee flew right in through the window and stung the Terrible Tragadabas.

He hollered—Oooouuuuu!—and jumped into the air.

Then he ran out the door and up the street as fast as his hairy legs could carry him.

He ran past the grandma. He ran past the big green tree. He disappeared over the hill with the bee stinging him at every step.

Then down from the high branch of the big green tree climbed Little Bitty.

Down from the higher branch climbed Middle Size.

Down from the highest branch climbed Great Big.

And down from the very tip top of the tree climbed . . . the storekeeper!

The bee came back and the store-keeper invited everyone inside to eat some . . . little cakes and honey!

COYOTE AND TURTLE

a Native American folktale
retold by Joe Hayes

Did you know that turtles are very brave animals? If you stop to think, you'll see they are. They never run away—not even from their fiercest enemies. And they certainly aren't afraid of Coyote.

One fine day in spring the turtles all decided to leave their home in the river and hunt for tender green cactus shoots. They all moved slowly up the river bank and out onto the desert, but Little Turtle, the youngest of the clan, moved the slowest of all.

Little Turtle had never been out of the river before and this new world was fascinating to him. He stopped to investigate each colorful rock or bush or clump of grass. His mother kept calling for him to hurry and catch up.

Then Little Turtle saw a patch of blue flowers. He wandered over to see them more closely, and when he looked up he realized that he was all alone.

Now, as I said, turtles are very brave, but this turtle was so young and this place was so strange that he began to cry—"hoo-hoo-hoo"—and turned to go home.

Little Turtle started back toward the river sobbing softly to himself, and who should happen by but Coyote. Coyote sat down and cocked his ear toward Little Turtle. Finally Coyote said, "Little Turtle, what a fine song you're singing!"

"I'm not singing," Little Turtle pouted. "I'm crying! Don't you know the difference between singing and crying?"

Coyote paid no attention. "Yes," he went on, "I know good music when I hear it. That is a fine song. Sing it a little louder for me."

"I told you I'm not singing. *I'm crying!*"

Now Coyote grew impatient. "Little Turtle, if you don't sing me your song good and loud, I'll swallow you whole."

That would be enough to frighten any other animal Little Turtle's size, but Little Turtle's mother had told him about Coyote. He knew what to do. He told Coyote, "Go on—swallow me. I'll bounce around in your stomach like a stone and kill you."

Coyote reached out a paw and touched Little Turtle's shell. It was hard as stone.

"Well, then," Coyote said, "I'll jump on you with all four feet and crush you!"

"Go ahead and try it. My shell is strong. It won't hurt me a bit. My mother told me so."

"What if I throw you against a rock?"

"The rock will break," Little Turtle said. "I won't feel a thing. My mother told me only one thing can hurt me."

Now Coyote changed his tone.

"Really?" he praised. "How strong you are! Only one thing can hurt you? Let me guess what it is: It must be Mountain Lion's sharp claws."

Little Turtle laughed, "Mountain Lion's claws will break on my shell."

"Then maybe it's Bear's powerful jaws?"

"Bear might as well try to crush a rock with his jaws. My shell will be harder."

"I give up, Little Turtle. Tell me what it is."

"My mother said that nothing can hurt me but the cold water of the river." Little Turtle shivered. "Oouuu! I hate cold water!"

Now Coyote laughed. "You foolish turtle. Since you hate water so much, that's just where I'll throw you!" And he picked Little Turtle up in his mouth and ran to the river and threw him into the water.

Little Turtle poked his head out of the water laughing. "Thank you, Coyote," he called out. "The river is where I live. You saved me a long walk back home." And Little Turtle swam away.

Coyote was so angry that he started to cry—"*Howw-ow-ow-ow . . .*"

A raven in a nearby tree heard Coyote and called down to him, "*Caw!* Coyote, what a beautiful song you're singing!! *Caw!*"

"Stupid bird!" Coyote screamed. "Don't you know the difference between singing and crying?"

EMILY'S HOUSE

by Niko Scharer
pictures by Joanne Fitzgerald

Emily lived in a little brick house
With a creaky old door and a little
brown mouse.
Emily listened, and Emily frowned
'Cause Emily heard two very
loud sounds!
For the door went creak
And the mouse went squeak
And Emily cried with a great big tear
And she said, "There's too much
noise in here!"

Well, Emily sighed, "Oh what to do?"
But the mouse said, "Get us a
pussycat too."

So Emily left in her white straw hat
And she came back home with a
tabby cat.
And the door went creak
And the mouse went squeak
And the cat meow-ed
And meow-ed so loud
That Emily cried with a great big tear
And she said, "There's too much
noise in here!"

Well, Emily sighed, "Oh what to do?"
But the mouse said, "Get us a puppy
dog too."

So Emily left with a jig and a jog
And she came back home with a
puppy dog.
And the door went creak
And the mouse went squeak
And the cat meow-ed
And the dog bow-wow-ed
And Emily cried with a great big tear
And she said, "There's too much
noise in here!"

Well, Emily sighed, "Oh what to do?"
But the mouse said, "Get us a black
sheep too."

So Emily left with a bounding leap
And she came back home with a
small black sheep.
And the door went creak
And the mouse went squeak
And the cat meow-ed

And the dog bow-wow-ed
And the sheep went baa
I want my maa
And Emily cried with a great big tear
And she said, "There's too much
noise in here!"

Well, Emily sighed, "Oh what to do?"
But the mouse said, "Get us a billy
goat too."

So Emily left with a five pound note
And she came back home with a
billy goat.
And the door went creak
And the mouse went squeak
And the cat meow-ed
And the dog bow-wow-ed
And the sheep went baa
And the goat went maa
And Emily cried with a great big tear

And she said, "There's too much noise in here!"

Well, Emily sighed, "Oh what to do?"
But the mouse said, "We need a brown cow too."

So Emily left, and I don't know how,
But she came back home with a big brown cow.
And the door went creak
And the mouse went squeak
And the cat meow-ed
And the dog bow-wow-ed
And the sheep went baa
And the goat went maa
And the cow went moo
And the noise just grew
And Emily cried with a great big tear
And she said, "There's too much noise in here!"

Well, Emily sighed, "Oh what to do?"
But the mouse said, "Get me a turtle dove too."

So Emily left with a push and a shove
And she came back home with a turtle dove.
And the door went creak
And the mouse went squeak
And the cat meow-ed
And the dog bow-wow-ed
And the sheep went baa
And the goat went maa
And the cow went moo
And the dove went coo
And Emily cried with a great big tear
And she yelled,

"THERE'S TOO MUCH NOISE IN HERE!"

Well, Emily didn't know what to do
But the mouse said, "Just try one thing new."

And he sent the cat and the dog and more
Why he sent all the animals out of the door.
And the door went creak
And the mouse went squeak
And Emily listened, and Emily smiled!
And she sighed the sigh of a happy child.

'Cause all she heard in her little brick house
Was a small sort of creak and the squeak of a mouse.

Caps for Sale

by Esphyr Slobodkina

A Tale of a Peddler, Some Monkeys and Their Monkey Business

Once there was a peddler who sold caps. But he was not like an ordinary peddler carrying his wares on his back. He carried them on top of his head.

First he had on his own checked cap, then a bunch of gray caps, then a bunch of brown caps, then a bunch of blue caps, and on the very top a bunch of red caps.

He walked up and down the streets, holding himself very straight so as not to upset his caps.

As he went along he called, "Caps! Caps for sale! Fifty cents a cap!"

One morning he couldn't sell any caps. He walked up the street and he walked down the street calling, "Caps! Caps for sale. Fifty cents a cap."

But nobody wanted any caps that morning. Nobody wanted even a red cap.

He began to feel very hungry, but he had no money for lunch.

"I think I'll go for a walk in the country," said he. And he walked out of town—slowly, slowly, so as not to upset his caps.

He walked for a long time until he came to a great big tree.

"That's a nice place for a rest," thought he.

And he sat down very slowly, under the tree and leaned back little by little against the tree-trunk so as not to disturb the caps on his head.

Then he put up his hand to feel if they were straight—first his own checked cap, then the gray caps, then the brown caps, then the blue caps, then the red caps on the very top.

They were all there.
So he went to sleep.
He slept for a long time.

When he woke up he was refreshed and rested.

But before standing up he felt with his hand to make sure his caps were in the right place.

All he felt was his own checked cap!

He looked to the right of him. No caps.

He looked to the left of him. No caps.

He looked in back of him. No caps.

He looked behind the tree. No caps.

Then he looked up into the tree. And what do you think he saw?

his foot, and he said, "You monkeys, you! You better give me back my caps!"

But the monkeys only stamped their feet back at him and said, "Tsz, tsz, tsz."

By this time the peddler was really very, very angry. He stamped both his feet and shouted, "You monkeys, you! You must give me back my caps!"

But the monkeys only stamped both their feet back at him and said, "Tsz, tsz, tsz."

On every branch sat a monkey. On every monkey was a gray, or a brown, or a blue, or a red cap!

The peddler looked at the monkeys.
The monkeys looked at the peddler.
He didn't know what to do.
Finally he spoke to them.
"You monkeys, you," he said, shaking a finger at them, "you give me back my caps."

But the monkeys only shook their fingers back at him and said, "Tsz, tsz, tsz."

This made the peddler angry, so he shook both hands at them and said, "You monkeys, you! You give me back my caps."

But the monkeys only shook both their hands back at him and said, "Tsz, tsz, tsz."

Now he felt quite angry. He stamped

At last he became so angry that he pulled off his own cap, threw it on the ground, and began to walk away.

But then, each monkey pulled off his cap . . .

and all the gray caps,
and all the brown caps,
and all the blue caps,
and all the red caps came flying down out of the tree.

So the peddler picked up his caps and put them back on his head—

first his own checked cap,
then the gray caps,
then the brown caps,
then the blue caps,
then the red caps on the very top.

And slowly, slowly, he walked back to town calling, "Caps! Caps for sale! Fifty cents a cap!"

Henny Penny

An English Tale
retold by Judy Sierra

One day Henny Penny was pecking corn in the cornyard when—whack!—something hit her on the head. "Goodness gracious me!" said Henny Penny. "The sky's a-going to fall. I must go and tell the king."

So she went along, and she went along, and she went along, till she met Cocky Locky. "Where are you going, Henny Penny?" asked Cocky Locky.

"Oh! I'm going to tell the king the sky's a-falling," said Henny Penny.

"May I come with you?" asked Cocky Locky.

"Certainly," said Henny Penny. So Henny Penny and Cocky Locky went to tell the king the sky was a-falling.

They went along, and they went along, and they went along, till they met Ducky Daddles. "Where are you going, Henny

Penny and Cocky Locky?" asked Ducky Daddles.

"Oh! We're going to tell the king the sky's a-falling," said Henny Penny and Cocky Locky.

"May I come with you?" asked Ducky Daddles.

"Certainly," said Henny Penny and Cocky Locky. So Henny Penny, Cocky Locky, and Ducky Daddles went to tell the king the sky was a-falling.

So they went along, and they went along, and they went along, till they met Goosey Loosey. "Where are you going, Henny Penny, Cocky Locky, and Ducky Daddles?" asked Goosey Loosey.

"Oh! We're going to tell the king the sky's a-falling," said Henny Penny and Cocky Locky and Ducky Daddles.

"May I come with you?" asked Goosey Loosey.

"Certainly!" said Henny Penny, Cocky Locky, and Ducky Daddles. So Henny Penny, Cocky Locky, Ducky Daddles, and Goosey Loosey went to tell the king the sky was a-falling.

So they went along, and they went along, and they went along, till they met Turkey Lurkey. "Where are you going, Henny Penny, Cocky Locky, Ducky Daddles, and Goosey Loosey?" asked Turkey Lurkey.

"Oh! We're going to tell the king the sky's a-falling," said Henny Penny, Cocky Locky, Ducky Daddles, and Goosey Loosey.

"May I come with you, Henny Penny, Cocky Locky, Ducky Daddles, and Goosey

Loosey?" asked Turkey Lurkey.

"Oh, certainly, Turkey Lurkey," said Henny Penny, Cocky Locky, Ducky Daddles, and Goosey Loosey. So Henny Penny, Cocky Locky, Ducky Daddles, Goosey Loosey, and Turkey Lurkey all went to tell the king the sky was a-falling.

So they went along, and they went along, and they went along, till they met Foxy Loxy, and Foxy Loxy said to Henny Penny, Cocky Locky, Ducky Daddles, Goosey Loosey, and Turkey Lurkey, "Where are you going, Henny Penny, Cocky Locky, Ducky Daddles, Goosey Loosey, and Turkey Lurkey?"

And Henny Penny, Cocky Locky, Ducky Daddles, Goosey Loosey, and Turkey Lurkey said to Foxy Loxy, "We're going to tell the king that the sky's a-falling."

"Then you will certainly want to use this shortcut," said Foxy Loxy. "Follow me!" And Foxy Loxy went into his den. Henny Penny, Cocky Locky, Ducky Daddles, Goosey Loosey, and Turkey Lurkey did not like the idea of going into such a dark cave, but finally Turkey Lurkey went in. And Goosey Loosey went in. And Ducky Daddles went in. And Cocky Locky went in.

"Cock-a-doodle-doo!" cried Cocky Locky. "Run, Henny Penny, run! Foxy Loxy will eat you . . ."

Henny Penny ran all the way home, and she never did get to tell the king that the sky was a-falling.

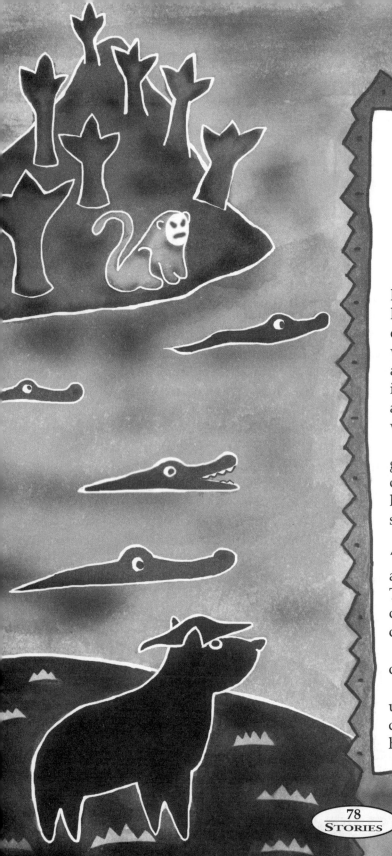

Counting Crocodiles

an Indonesian folktale

retold by Judy Sierra

Once, Mouse-Deer wanted to visit his friend Monkey. Now, Monkey lived on another island, and the two of them would visit when the tide was very low—they would scamper along the sand between the two islands. But today the tide was high, and what was even worse, the water was full of crocodiles!

Mouse-Deer had an idea. He grabbed a dry leaf that looked like a crown and put it on his head. Then he stood on a high rock next to the shore.

"Listen, crocodiles!" he shouted. "Attention all crocodiles. I bring you a royal proclamation from our king. The king has declared that all crocodiles living in this sea must be counted!"

"Why does he want us to be counted?" asked an old crocodile.

"Because . . . oh . . . because he is uh . . . going to invite all of you to dinner, yes, and he wants to know how much food he should prepare for you," answered Mouse-Deer.

The crocodiles looked at Mouse-Deer as if they thought he would make a fine dinner himself. But the idea of being invited to the royal palace for dinner was so wonderful that they went off to round up all their friends and relatives.

When he saw all the crocodiles swimming and thrashing in the sea before him, Mouse-Deer asked, "How shall I ever count you all? There are so many of you, and you move about so much."

Then he thought a bit and said, "Why don't you all form a long line . . . yes . . . form a long line from here, all the way to that island over there. Then I will be able to count you."

The crocodiles formed a long line, head to tail, stretching from the place where Mouse-Deer stood all the way to the island. Mouse-Deer then jumped from crocodile to crocodile, counting as he went, "One, two, three, four, five, six, seven."

Then he hopped off the last crocodile and onto the island.

"*You* will all be receiving your dinner invitations soon!" he called out to the crocodiles. "Good bye!"

Then Mouse-Deer trotted into the jungle to find his friend Monkey.

THE STRONGEST ONE OF ALL

A Russian Folktale

retold by Mirra Ginsburg
pictures by Jose Aruego and Ariane Dewey

A lamb slipped on the ice and cried, "Ice, ice, you made me fall. Are you strong? Are you the strongest one of all?"

But the ice answered, "If I were the strongest, would the sun melt me?"

The lamb went to the sun and asked, "Sun, sun, are you the strongest one of all?"

But the sun answered, "If I were the strongest, would the cloud cover me?"

The lamb went to the cloud and asked, "Cloud, cloud, are you the strongest one of all?"

But the cloud answered, "If I were the strongest, would I scatter into rain?"

The lamb went to the rain and asked, "Rain, rain, are you the strongest one of all?"

But the rain answered, "If I were the strongest, would the earth swallow me?"

The lamb went to the earth and asked, "Earth, earth, are you the strongest one of all?"

But the earth answered, "If I were the strongest, would the grass push its roots down through me, push its shoots up through me?"

The lamb went to the grass and asked, "Grass, grass, are you the strongest one of all?"

But the grass answered, "If I were the strongest, would a lamb pluck me, would a lamb eat me?"

And the lamb leaped with joy. "I may slip, and I may fall, but I'm the strongest! I'm the strongest of them all!"

Rattlesnake, Mouse, and Coyote

A Mexican Tale
retold by Judy Sierra

Mouse was running across the mesa, scurrying between the stones, looking for seeds to eat.

"Help! Help!" A tiny voice, faraway and muffled, called from under a nearby rock. Mouse stopped running and listened. "Please let me out!" the voice cried. "Roll this stone over and let me out!"

Mouse pushed the rock with his paws and nudged it with his nose. At last, the rock rolled aside. Out came Rattlesnake, hissing and shaking his tail rattles. As soon as he saw Mouse, he grabbed Mouse tightly in his coils.

"Let me go!" cried Mouse. "It was I who moved the rock aside to let you out. I saved your life."

"You saved my life because you are a kindhearted mouse. I am going to eat you because I am a hungry rattlesnake," Rattlesnake replied.

"But you should be grateful and spare my life. If it weren't for me, you would still be trapped under that rock."

"Rattlesnakes are not grateful," said the rattlesnake.

Just then, Señor Coyote came trotting along. "Hey! Cousin!" cried Mouse. "Is this fair? I saved Rattlesnake's life, and now he is going to eat me."

"What?" asked Coyote. "How did this happen?"

"Rattlesnake was trapped in a hole under that rock," said Mouse. "I rolled the rock aside and let him out. I saved his life, and now he wants to eat me."

"No one says rattlesnakes have to be grateful," said Rattlesnake. "I'm hungry, because I was under that rock for so long."

"I don't understand. This doesn't make sense," said Coyote. "You say Mouse was under the rock?"

"No, I was under the rock!" hissed Rattlesnake.

"Oh, my poor brains," said Coyote. "I can't understand at all . . . . Rattlesnake rolled the rock off Mouse. . . ."

"NO! Mouse rolled the rock off me!"

"I just can't understand at all. Please be so kind as to show me exactly what happened."

"I was in here," said Rattlesnake, letting go of Mouse and crawling back into the hole.

"And this rock was on top of you?" asked Coyote, pushing the rock back on top of Rattlesnake.

"Yes! Yes! Now let me out!" came Rattlesnake's small voice from under the rock.

"I will leave that up to Mouse," answered Coyote as he trotted away.

The Town Mouse & the Country Mouse

retold by Lorinda Bryan Cauley

The Country Mouse lived by himself in a snug little hole in an old log in a field of wild flowers.

One day he decided to invite his cousin the Town Mouse for a visit, and he sent him a letter.

When his cousin arrived, the Country Mouse could hardly wait to show him around. They went for a walk, and on the way they gathered a basket of acorns.

They picked some wild wheat stalks.

They stopped by the river and sat on the bank, cooling their feet.

And on the way home for supper, they picked some wild flowers for the house.

The Country Mouse settled his cousin in an easy chair with a cup of fresh mint tea and then went about preparing the best country supper he had to offer.

He made a delicious soup of barley and corn.

He simmered a root stew seasoned with thyme.

Then he made a rich nutcake for dessert, which he would serve hot from the oven.

The Town Mouse watched in amazement. He had never seen anyone work so hard.

But when they sat down to eat, the Town Mouse only picked and nibbled at the food on his plate. Finally, turning up his long nose, he said, "I cannot understand, Cousin, how you can work so hard and put up with food such as this. Why, you live no better than the ants and work twice as hard."

"It may be simple food," said the Country Mouse, "but there is plenty of it. And there is nothing I enjoy more than gathering everything fresh from the fields and cooking a hot supper."

"I should die of boredom," the Town Mouse complained. "I never have to work for my supper, and in my life there is hardly ever a dull moment."

"I can't imagine any other life," answered the Country Mouse.

"In that case, dear Cousin, come back to town with me and see what you have been missing."

So, out of curiosity, the Country Mouse agreed to go. Off they went, scampering across fields while avoiding the cows and down a dirt lane, edged with bright flowers, until at last they reached the cobblestones leading into town.

The streetlights flickered eerily, and with each horse and carriage that clip-clopped by, the Country Mouse trembled with fear.

At last they reached a row of elegant town houses, their windows glowing in lamplight. "This is where I live," said the Town Mouse. The Country Mouse had to admit that it looked warm and inviting.

They went inside and crept past the ticktock of the grandfather clock in the hall and into the living room. The Town Mouse led his cousin to a small entrance hole behind the wood basket next to the fireplace.

Once inside, the Town Mouse lit a candle and started a fire. The Country Mouse looked around the room. It was so much grander than his little hole in the old log. Why, his cousin's bed was covered with a fine silk handkerchief as a bedspread.

They had been traveling all day, and the Country Mouse was tired and hungry. So he was surprised when his cousin started to go back through the entrance hole. "Could we have something to eat before you show me around?" he asked timidly.

"But of course," said his cousin. "That is where we are going. To have a feast of a supper."

They went through the living room and into the dining room and there on a large table were the remains of a fine supper. The Country Mouse's eyes were wide with astonishment. He had never seen so much food all at once, nor so many kinds.

"Help yourself," invited the Town Mouse. "Whatever you like is yours for the taking."

The Country Mouse scampered across the starched white linen and stared at the dishes. Creamy puddings, cheeses, biscuits and chocolate candies. Cakes, jellies, fresh fruit and nuts!

It all looked and smelled delicious. He hardly knew where to begin.

He took a sip from a tall, sparkling glass and thought, "This is heaven. Maybe I have been wrong to have wasted my life in the country."

He had just started nibbling on a piece of strawberry cake when suddenly the dining room doors flew open and two servants came in to clear away the dishes.

The two mice scampered off the table and hid beneath it. When they heard the doors close again, the Town Mouse coaxed his cousin back onto the table to eat what was left.

But they had hardly taken two bites when the doors opened again and a small girl in her nightdress ran in to look for her doll, which had fallen under the table. This time the Town Mouse hid behind the jug of cream and the Country Mouse crouched in terror behind the butter dish. But she didn't see them.

As soon as the girl was gone, the Town Mouse began to eat again. But the Country Mouse stood listening. "Come on," said his cousin. "Relax and enjoy this delicious cheese."

But before the Country Mouse could even taste it, he heard barking and growling outside the door. "Wha-, what's that?" he stammered.

"It is only the dogs of the house," answered the Town Mouse. "Don't worry. They're not allowed in the dining room." And with that, the doors burst open and in bounded two roaring dogs. This time the mice scampered down the side of the table, out of the room, and back to the hole in the living room just in the nick of time.

"Cousin, you may live in luxury here, but I'd rather eat my simple supper in the country than a feast like this in fear for my life. I'm going home right away," said the Country Mouse.

"*Yes*, I suppose that the hectic life of the town is not for everybody, but it's what makes me happy. If you ever need a little excitement in your life, you can come for another visit," replied his cousin.

"And any time you want a little peace and quiet and healthy food, come and visit me in the country," said the Country Mouse.

Then off he went to his snug little home in the fields, whistling a tune and looking forward to a good book by the fire and a mug of hot barley-corn soup.

THE Shoemaker AND THE Elves

retold by Anne Rockwell

A shoemaker had become so poor that he had only enough leather for one pair of shoes. In the evening he cut out the leather for the shoes he would make next morning, and then he went to bed. But in the morning, when he was about to go to work, the pair of shoes stood all finished on his cobbler's bench. When he saw them, the shoemaker was very surprised, and did not know what to think. And when he looked closely at the shoes, he saw there was not one bad stitch in them; they were perfect in every way.

Before long, a customer came into his shop and bought the shoes. But because they were so beautiful and so well made the customer paid extra for them, and the shoemaker was able to buy leather for two pairs of shoes.

He cut them out at night, and woke up early to sew the shoes together, but once again, there was no need to do so. For when he got up, the shoes were already made. Customers came, too, and he made enough

money that day to buy leather for four pairs of shoes. Again next morning he found the four pairs of shoes made, and so it went on—what leather he cut in the evening was finished by morning, and the shoes were always perfect and well made, so the shoemaker became a rich man.

One winter evening, when the man had finished cutting out the leather, he said to his wife, "What if we were to stay up tonight and see who it is that helps us so?"

His wife liked that idea, and so the two of them hid themselves in a corner of the shop, and waited and watched.

When it was exactly midnight, two little elves came. They sat down promptly on the cobbler's bench, took the cutout leather, and began to stitch and began to sew and began to hammer. And all this they did so nimbly and so well that the shoemaker could not turn his eyes away for amazement. The two little elves did not stop working until the shoes were all done. Then quickly and quietly they ran away.

Next morning the woman said, "Those little elves have made us rich, and we should show them that we are grateful for it. They run about so without any clothes on. They must be cold. I will make them each a little hat and shirt and vest and trousers, and I will knit them each a pair of stockings. And you can make two little pairs of shoes."

"I will be happy to," said the shoemaker.

A few nights later they laid their presents on the cobbler's bench in place of the cutout leather and hid themselves where they could watch the two little elves.

At midnight the little elves came bounding in, ready to go to work at once. They were very surprised to find no cutout leather, only the pretty little clothes. They touched the little vests and hats and shirts and trousers, the striped stockings and leather shoes. Suddenly they smiled with delight when they realized the clothes were theirs. They dressed themselves quickly and sang:

"We are boys so fine to see,
Why should we now cobblers be?"

Then they danced and skipped off the cobbler's bench and around the shop and out the door. From then on they came no more, but the shoemaker and his wife lived happily and well.

Jamaica's Find

Juanita Havill
Illustrations by
Anne Sibley O'Brien

When Jamaica arrived at the park, there was no one there. It was almost supper time, but she still had a few minutes to play.

She sat in a swing, pushed off with her toes, and began pumping. It was fun not to have to watch out for the little ones who always ran in front of the swings.

Then she climbed up the slide. There was a red sock hat on the ladder step. Jamaica took it for a ride. She slid down so fast that she fell in the sand and lay flat on her back.

When she rolled over to get up, she saw a stuffed dog beside her. It was a cuddly gray dog, worn from hugging. All over it were faded food and grass stains. Its button nose must have fallen off. There was a round white spot in its place. Two black ears hung from its head.

Jamaica put the dog in her bicycle basket.

She took the hat into the park house and gave it to the young man at the counter.

The first thing her mother said when Jamaica came in the door was: "Where did that dog come from?"

"The park. I stopped to play on the way home," Jamaica said. "I found someone's red hat and took it to the Lost and Found."

"But, Jamaica, you should have returned the dog, too," said her mother.

Then she said, "I'm glad you returned the hat."

"It didn't fit me," Jamaica said.

"Maybe the dog doesn't fit you either," her mother said.

"I like the dog," said Jamaica.

"Don't put that silly dog on the table!" Jamaica's brother said.

"You don't know where it came from. It isn't very clean, you know," her father said.

"Not in the kitchen, Jamaica," her mother said.

Jamaica took the dog to her room. She could hear her mother say, "It probably belongs to a girl just like Jamaica."

After dessert Jamaica went to her room very quietly. She held the dog up and looked at it closely. Then she tossed it on a chair.

"Jamaica," her mother called from the kitchen. "Have you forgotten? It's your turn to dry the dishes."

"Do I have to, Mother? I don't feel good," Jamaica answered.

Jamaica heard the pots rattle. Then she heard her mother's steps.

Her mother came in quietly, sat down by Jamaica, and looked at the stuffed dog, which lay alone on the chair. She didn't say anything. After a while she put her arms around Jamaica and squeezed for a long time.

"Mother, I want to take the dog back to the park," Jamaica said.

"We'll go first thing in the morning." Her mother smiled.

Jamaica ran to the park house and plopped the stuffed dog on the counter.

"I found this by the slide," she told the young man.

"Oh, hi. Aren't you the girl who gave me the hat last night?"

"Yes," said Jamaica, feeling hot around her ears.

"You sure do find a lot of things. I'll put it on the Lost and Found shelf."

Jamaica stood watching him.

"Is that all?" he asked. "You didn't find anything else, did you?"

"No. That's all." She stayed to watch him put the dog on a shelf behind him.

"I'm sure some little girl or boy will come in after it today, a nice little dog like that," the young man said.

Jamaica ran outside. She didn't feel like playing alone. There was no one else at the park but her mother, who sat on a bench. Then Jamaica saw a girl and her mother cross the street to the park.

"Hi. I'm Jamaica. What's your name?" she said to the girl.

The girl let go of her mother's hand. "Kristin," she said.

"Do you want to climb the jungle gym with me, Kristin?" Jamaica said.

Kristin ran toward Jamaica. "Yes, but I have to find something first."

"What?" asked Jamaica. Kristin was bending under the slide.

"What did you lose?" said Jamaica.

"Edgar dog. I brought him with me yesterday and now I can't find him," Kristin answered.

"Was he kind of gray with black ears?" Jamaica couldn't keep from shouting. "Come along with me."

The young man in the park house looked over the counter at the two girls.

"Now what have you found?" he asked Jamaica.

But this time Jamaica didn't drop anything onto the counter. Instead, she smiled her biggest smile. "I found the girl who belongs to that stuffed dog."

Jamaica was almost as happy as Kristin, who took Edgar dog in her arms and gave him a big welcome-back hug.

The Rooster Who Went to His Uncle's Wedding

a Latin American folktale
retold by Alma Flor Ada
illustrated by Kathleen Kuchera

Early one morning, when the sun had not yet appeared, the rooster of this story was busy shining his beak and combing up his feathers. It was the day of his uncle's wedding, and the rooster wanted to be on time.

   When everything looked perfect he set off down the road with a brisk and springy walk. With each step the rooster nodded his head, thinking of all the wonderful things waiting for him at the wedding banquet.

Before long his stomach began to growl. "I wish I'd eaten breakfast," he said. Then something caught his eye. There, next to the road, sat a single golden kernel of corn.

Perfect, the rooster thought. But when he got closer he could see that the kernel was lying in a puddle of mud. If he ate it he would get his beak all dirty.

Oh, that rooster was hungry. But he couldn't go to his uncle's wedding with a dirty beak. *What to do? Peck or not peck?* he wondered.

The rooster stared at the kernel.

Then with one sharp peck he gobbled it down . . . and wound up with a beak full of mud.

So the rooster looked around quickly for someone who could help him. First he noticed the grass growing on the side of the road.

The rooster said to the grass:
"Dear grass, velvety grass,
won't you please clean my beak
so that I can go to my own uncle's wedding?"

But the grass answered:
"No, I won't. Why should I?"

The rooster looked around to see if there was anyone else who could help him. Just then he saw a lamb grazing in the field. Maybe he could *scare* the grass into helping. So he asked the lamb:
"Dear lamb, woolly lamb,
please eat the grass
that won't clean my beak
so that I can go to my own uncle's wedding."

But the lamb answered:
"No, I won't. Why should I?"

The rooster strutted back and forth in dismay. But then he saw a dog walking on the road. So he asked the dog:
"Dear dog, fierce dog,
please bite the lamb
that won't eat the grass
that won't clean my beak
so that I can go to my own uncle's wedding."

But the dog answered:
"No, I won't. Why should I?"

Well, this rooster was not one to give up. So he went over to a stick lying by the road. And he asked it:
"Dear stick, hard stick,
please hit the dog
that won't bite the lamb
that won't eat the grass
that won't clean my beak
so that I can go to my own uncle's wedding."

But the stick answered:
"No, I won't. Why should I?"

The rooster was starting to worry. But he looked around for someone else to help, and he spotted a campfire the shepherds had lit. He got close to the fire and asked:
"Dear fire, bright fire,
please burn the stick
that won't hit the dog
that won't bite the lamb
that won't eat the grass
that won't clean my beak
so that I can go to my own uncle's wedding."

But the fire answered:
"No, I won't. Why should I?"

The rooster ruffled his feathers and paced. Would anyone be able to help

him in time? Then he noticed a brook crossing the field. He bent over and whispered, as sincerely as he could:

"Dear water, clear water,
please put out the fire
that won't burn the stick
that won't hit the dog
that won't bite the lamb
that won't eat the grass
that won't clean my beak
so that I can go to my own uncle's wedding."

But the water answered:

"No, I won't. Why should I?"

Now the poor rooster couldn't think of anyone else to ask for help. He lifted his muddy beak up and crowed. But then he noticed that the sun was beginning to appear among the clouds. And he said:

"Dear sun, my good friend,
please dry out the water
that won't put out the fire
that won't burn the stick
that won't hit the dog
that won't bite the lamb
that won't eat the grass
that won't clean my beak
so that I can go to my own uncle's wedding."

And the sun answered:

"Of course I will. Every morning you greet me with your bright song, my friend. I will gladly dry out the water."

But then the water cried out:

"No, please don't dry me out. I will put out the fire."

And the fire cried out:

"No, please don't put me out. I will burn the stick."

The stick, in turn, cried out:

"No, please don't burn me. I will hit the dog."

But the dog cried out:

"No, please don't hit me. I will bite the lamb."

So the lamb quickly cried out:

"No, please don't bite me. I will eat the grass."

But the grass cried out very loudly:

"No, please don't eat me. I will clean the rooster's beak."

And before you know it the rooster's beak shone as bright as the day.

So the rooster said good-bye to everyone with a happy "Cock-a-doodle-doo!" and went on his way to his uncle's wedding. And he walked with a brisk and springy walk, to get there on time for the banquet.

GRANDFATHER AND I

Helen E. Buckley
illustrated by Jan Ormerod

Grandfather and I are going for a walk.
It will be a slow walk because
Grandfather and I never hurry.
We walk along and walk along
and stop . . . and look . . . just as long as we like.

Other people we know are always in a hurry.
Mothers hurry.
They walk in a hurry and talk in a hurry.
And they always want **you** to hurry.

But Grandfather and I never hurry.
We walk along and walk along
and stop . . . and look . . . just as long as we like.

Fathers hurry.
They hurry off to work and then they hurry home again.
They hurry when they kiss you
and when they take you for a ride.

But Grandfather and I never hurry.
We walk along and walk along
and stop . . . and look . . . just as long as we like.

Brothers and sisters hurry too.
They go so fast they often bump into you.
And when they take you for a walk
they are always leaving you far behind.

But Grandfather and I never hurry.
We walk along and walk along
and stop . . . and look . . . just as long as we like.

Things hurry.
Cars and buses. Trains and little boats.
They make noises when they hurry—
they toot whistles and blow horns.
And sometimes scare you.

But Grandfather and I never hurry.
We walk along and walk along
and stop . . . and look . . . just as long as
we like.

And when Grandfather and I get
home,
we sit in a chair and rock and rock . . .
and read a little . . .
and talk a little . . .
and look . . . just as long as we like—

until somebody tells us to hurry.

The Three Little Pigs

retold by Anne Rockwell

Once upon a time there was an old sow with three little pigs, and she sent them out into the world to seek their fortune.

The first little pig met a man with a bundle of straw and said to him, "Please, man, give me that straw to build a house." And the man did, and the little pig built a house with the straw.

Along came a wolf who knocked at the door and said, "Little pig, little pig, let me come in."

And the little pig answered, "No, no, by the hair of my chinny, chin, chin!"

So the wolf said, "Then I'll huff and I'll puff and I'll blow your house in!"

So the wolf huffed and he puffed and he blew the house in and ate up the little pig.

The second little pig met a man with a bundle of sticks and said to him, "Please, man, give me those sticks to build a house." And the man did, and the little pig built a house with the sticks.

Then, along came the wolf who knocked at the door and said, "Little pig, little pig, let me come in."

And the little pig answered, "No, no, by the hair of my chinny, chin, chin!"

So the wolf said, "Then I'll huff and I'll puff and I'll blow your house in!"

So the wolf huffed and he puffed, and he puffed and he huffed, and he blew the house down and ate up the little pig.

The third little pig met a man with a load of bricks and said to him, "Please, man, give me those bricks to build a house." And the man gave him the bricks, and the little pig built a house with them.

Then the wolf came, just as he had to the other little pigs, and knocked on the door and said, "Little pig, little pig, let me come in."

And the little pig answered, "No, no, by the hair of my chinny, chin, chin!"

So the wolf said, "Then I'll huff and I'll puff and I'll blow your house in!"

Well, the wolf huffed and puffed, and he puffed and he huffed, and he huffed and he puffed, but he could not blow that house down. So when he found that he could not, he said, "Little pig, I know where there are some nice turnips."

"Where?" said the little pig.

"Down in Farmer Smith's field," said the wolf. "If you will be ready tomorrow morning at six o'clock, I will come and get you, and we can go together to pick some turnips for dinner."

"Very well," said the little pig, and the wolf went away.

The next morning the little pig got up at five o'clock and picked the turnips and got back home before the wolf came to get him at six.

When the wolf arrived, he said, "Little pig, are you ready?"

The little pig said, "I have been there and back, and I have a nice potful of turnips for dinner."

The wolf felt very angry at this, but he said in his nicest voice, "Little pig, I know where there is a fine apple tree."

"Where?" said the little pig.

"Over in Mary's garden," said the wolf. "And if you will not trick me, I will come for you tomorrow morning at five o'clock, and we will pick some apples."

Well, the little pig got up next morning at four o'clock and went off for apples, hoping to get home before the wolf came for him. But he had farther to go this time, and he had to climb the tree besides, so just as he

was climbing down the tree, he saw the wolf coming, and this frightened the little pig very much.

The wolf stood under the tree and said, "Why, little pig! Are you here before me? Are they nice apples?"

"Oh, yes," said the little pig, "they are good and sweet. Here, I will throw one down to you."

And he threw the apple so far that while the wolf was running off to get it, the little pig jumped down from the tree and ran all the way home.

Next day the wolf came again, and said to the little pig, "Little pig, there is a fair in town this afternoon. Will you go with me?"

"Oh, yes," said the little pig, "I will. What time will you come to get me?"

"I will come at three," said the wolf.

So the little pig left early, as usual, and bought a butter churn at the fair. He was walking home with it when he saw the wolf coming. The little pig did not know what to do. So he got inside the butter churn to hide. While he was squeezing himself in, he turned the butter churn around on its side, and it rolled down the hill with the little pig inside. And it rolled right down the hill towards the wolf, and the wolf was so frightened that he ran home without ever going to the fair.

Later he went to the little pig's house and told him about the big scary thing that had come rolling down the hill to chase him.

Then the little pig said, "Ha! So I scared you, did I? That was only the butter churn I bought at the fair, and I was inside."

When he heard this the wolf was very, very angry indeed, and he declared that he would eat up that little pig, and he was coming down the chimney to get him.

As soon as the little pig heard this, he filled up a large pot with water and built up a blazing fire. Just as the wolf was coming down the chimney the little pig took the lid off the pot, and in fell the wolf.

The little pig popped the lid back on the pot, boiled up the wolf, ate him for supper, and lived happily ever after.

Anansi and the Biggest, Sweetest Melon

an African tale

For weeks Anansi had been sitting in his tree, dreaming about the sweet melons growing in Elephant's garden.

"If you love melons so much, why don't you grow them yourself?" his wife asked.

"Grow them myself?" Anansi asked. "Why should I when Elephant will grow them for me?"

Anansi's wife shook her head at her lazy husband. "He is not growing them for you. He is growing them for himself."

"That's what he thinks," Anansi said with a laugh. And then he went back to his dreaming.

Each day the hot sun and the cold rain helped the melons grow bigger and sweeter, until finally they were ready. Anansi wouldn't have wasted a minute, but he knew that Elephant would not want to share his melons. So he waited. And waited. And waited. Finally, one day Elephant was so hot and tired from working in his garden that he lumbered back to his house to take a nap.

Right away, Anansi swung down from the tree and used a broken thorn to make a hole in the biggest, sweetest melon he could find. Then he squeezed inside and began eating. He ate and ate and ate, until he could eat no more.

"I'll go back home now," he said to himself. But when he tried to squeeze through the hole, he discovered that he had grown too fat to get out!

Anansi sat down with a thud. Was he going to be stuck in this melon forever? Just then, Elephant returned to the garden and chose the biggest, sweetest melon to eat for himself. Unfortunately, Anansi was inside.

Anansi didn't have much time. Suddenly, he got an idea.

"Put me down," he cried as Elephant carried the melon toward his house.

Elephant was startled. "Who said that?" he asked, looking all around.

"I did," said Anansi from inside the melon.

Elephant scratched his head. "I didn't know that melons could talk."

"This one can," Anansi said.

"A talking melon," Elephant said, scratching his head again. "I must show it to the king."

And so Elephant ran down the road as fast as his legs could carry him. On the way he bumped into Rhinoceros.

"Where are you taking that melon?" Rhinoceros asked.

"To the king."

"To the king?"

"Yes. To the king. This is a talking melon."

"A talking melon?" Rhinoceros laughed. "That is the silliest thing I ever heard."

"Not half as silly as you," Anansi said from inside the melon.

Rhinoceros started to shake angrily. "Why did you say that, Elephant?"

"I didn't," replied Elephant. "It was the melon."

"In that case, I will go with you to the king."

So the two of them ran down the road as fast as their legs could carry them. On the way they bumped into Gorilla.

"Where are you taking that melon?" Gorilla asked.

"To the king."

"To the king?"

"Yes. To the king. This is a talking melon."

"A talking melon?" Gorilla laughed. "That is the silliest thing I ever heard."

"Not half as silly as you," Anansi said from inside the melon.

Gorilla started to shake angrily. "Why did you say that, Elephant?"

"I didn't," replied Elephant. "It was the melon."

"In that case, I will go with you to the king."

So the three of them ran down the road as fast as their legs could carry them. On the way they bumped into Turtle.

"Where are you taking that melon?" Turtle asked.

"To the king."

"To the king?"

"Yes. To the king. This is a talking melon."

"A talking melon?" Turtle laughed. "That is the silliest thing I ever heard."

"Not half as silly as you," Anansi said from inside the melon.

Turtle started to shake angrily. "Why did you say that, Elephant?"

"I didn't," replied Elephant. "It was the melon."

"In that case, I will go with you to the king."

So the four of them ran down the road as fast as their legs could carry them. Finally, they reached the home of the king, Lion.

"Why are you all running with that melon?" Lion asked.

"We wanted to show it to you," they replied.

"Did you think I never saw a melon before?"

"Not one that talks," they replied.

"A talking melon?" Lion laughed. "That is the silliest thing I ever heard."

"Not half as silly as you," Anansi said from inside the melon.

Lion started to shake angrily. "How dare you talk to a king like that?" He grabbed the melon and threw it all the way back to Elephant's garden. The melon bounced and broke open into two halves.

Anansi climbed out of one of the broken halves and up to his house in the tree. He yawned, closed his eyes, and was soon fast asleep, dreaming about all the melons he would eat that summer.

107
STORIES

The Fearsome Beast

a Masai tale *retold by Judy Sierra*

One morning, a little caterpillar crawled into the hollow log that was Rabbit's house. Rabbit was away, and when he returned he saw the marks of Caterpillar's feet on the ground and he cried out, "Who is in my house?"

Caterpillar answered in a loud voice (and the hollow log made it even louder), "I am a great warrior, son of the long one! I crush the rhinoceros to the earth, and I make dust of the elephant. I am invincible!"

Rabbit was afraid, and he said to himself, "What can a small animal like myself do against a warrior who tramples the elephant into dust?" So Rabbit called on Leopard to come and help him.

Leopard came, and growled fiercely, and said, "Who is in the house of my friend Rabbit?"

Caterpillar answered, "I am a great warrior, son of the long one!

I crush the rhinoceros to the earth, and I make dust of the elephant. I am invincible!"

Leopard backed off, saying, "If he crushes the elephant and the rhinoceros, he will do the same to me!" And Leopard went away.

Next, Rabbit called on Rhinoceros, but when Rhinoceros heard what Caterpillar had to say, he cried, "What? He can crush me to the earth? I'd better leave here fast!"

Rabbit then tried Elephant, asking him to please rid his house of this monster. But when Elephant heard the caterpillar's boast, he told Rabbit that he had no desire to be trampled underfoot like dust, and stomped away.

Now, Frog had been sitting under a leaf nearby, watching and listening to everything that had happened. Frog went up to Rabbit's door and asked who was inside.

Caterpillar replied, "I am a great warrior, son of the long one! I crush the rhinoceros to the earth, and I make dust of the elephant. I am invincible!"

Frog went right up to the hollow log and said in a great, loud voice of his own, "Borooommm! Borooommm! I am the mighty leaper! The ground splits where I sit, and the Creator has made me green, slimy, and vile!"

When Caterpillar heard this, he trembled and said, "But I am only a caterpillar! Please, don't hurt me!"

Rabbit and Frog dragged Caterpillar out of the house, and they laughed and laughed at all the trouble he had caused everyone.

The Ants and the Grasshopper

Aesop

One beautiful spring morning, as Grasshopper was dancing and playing music on his fiddle, he bumped into some ants working in their garden. They were busy hoeing dirt, planting seeds, and watering the little green shoots that had begun to poke their heads above the earth.

"Why are you working on such a beautiful spring day?" Grasshopper asked. "That can wait. A day like this is for dancing and playing music, not for working in the sun."

The ants didn't even stop to rest as they explained to Grasshopper that they were planting a garden so they would have food for winter.

"That's ridiculous," said Grasshopper. "There's plenty to eat." And he pointed to the green leaves and the grass and the flowers that were blooming everywhere under the warm spring sun.

"Spring doesn't last forever," replied the ants. And then they got right back to work without even listening to what Grasshopper had to say.

Grasshopper laughed at their silliness. He twirled himself around and around, and played his fiddle long into the evening, and into the evening after that, and the evening after that.

Spring turned to summer, and Grasshopper still played his fiddle as the ants worked under the hot sun. They watered their plants, pulled out the weeds, and raked the soil.

When fall came, Grasshopper still merrily played his fiddle as the air turned chilly and the leaves fell from the trees. The ants quietly harvested their vegetables and fruits and dragged them into their home beneath the ground.

Finally winter came howling from the north and snow covered the ground. Inside their home, the ants were warm and had plenty of food. Outside in the icy wind, Grasshopper wandered everywhere searching for leaves and blades of grass. But no matter how long he looked, he couldn't find a thing to eat. He was cold and hungry and frightened, and didn't feel like playing music any more.

One day, cold and shivering, Grasshopper knocked at the ants' door. "Who's there?" they asked.

"It is me," said Grasshopper weakly.

The ants opened the door to see Grasshopper shivering in the cold north wind. "I'm cold and hungry," said Grasshopper. "May I come in and have something to eat?"

The ants looked at him. All through the spring and summer and fall they had worked and worked, while Grasshopper did nothing but play his fiddle and dance. But in spite of his laziness, they felt sorry for him. Finally, one of the ants said, "We will be glad to let you in, if you promise to help us in the garden next year."

"I will help you," Grasshopper promised.

So all winter long, Grasshopper lived comfortably with the ants, eating the food that they had worked so hard to grow all spring and summer and fall.

When spring came again, Grasshopper kept his promise, working all day long with the ants. But sometimes at night, after the digging and hoeing and watering was done, he would take his fiddle out and play music for his friends. He had learned that it is best to work first and play when the work is done.

Muffin was so busy listening to the noise in the Sea Shell he did not hear the great scuttling crab coming down the beach. Then the crab scuttled up and nearly pinched Muffin's little foot. But Muffin grabbed the old crab by the back and threw him in the Sea.

Then Muffin took a big drink of Sea Water. But he didn't like it. Why was that?

So he walked along in the warm soft sand. And he saw more crabs and pink shells and white shells and jellyfish and an old brown bottle.

At sundown Muffin heard the dinner bell. So he went back on the boat and they had crab soup for supper. Then it was night.

It was night and Muffin didn't hear a thing but the gentle lapping of waves around the boat. The moon and the stars shone down on the Sea. And you could see their lights on the waters. But could Muffin hear that?

The fish swam slowly about the Sea.
But could Muffin hear that?
And lobsters crawled into lobster pots down in the depths of the Sea.
But could Muffin hear that?
And a giant shark swam round and round.
But could Muffin hear that?
And a swordfish.
But could Muffin hear that?
And some tiny little fish.
But could Muffin hear that?
And all around under the boat were starfish and barnacles and flounders and periwinkles and whales.
But could Muffin hear that?

Then in the morning they went fishing.
Flip flop the Captain caught a fish.
Flip flop flip flop it jumped on the bottom of the boat.
It was a mackerel!
Flip flop flip flop Muffin caught a fish.
Flip flop flip flop it jumped on the bottom of the boat.
It was a flounder!
Flip flop flip flop the Captain caught another fish.
It was a codfish!

Then all of a sudden there was a BIG SPLASHING in the water near the boat.
What could it be?
It was not a whale.
Was it the sun falling out of the sky? *NO*
Was it a walrus blowing through his whiskers? *NO*
Was it a sea horse galloping? *NO*
Was it a little shrimp? *NO*
What do you think it was?

It was Muffin. Swimming and splashing in the Sea. *Ho! Ho!* said the Captain as he pulled Muffin out of the water. *I think I've caught a dogfish this time.*

A House by the Sea

by *Joanne Ryder*
pictures by *Melissa Sweet*

If I could live in a little house,
I'd live in a house by the sea.
Some days I'd visit the
frisky seals,
and some days they'd visit me.

We'd walk in the rain,
those seals and I,
till we'd stop for a slice
of fish-eyed pie.

When I got too wet
or they got too dry,
we'd hug and we'd run
and we'd yell, "Good-bye."

I'd watch and I'd wave
to those seals in the sea,
and their flippers would splash,
waving back at me.

If I could live in a little house,
I'd live in a house by the sea.
And I'd whisper at night
when the moon was bright,
"Would you please give a wish
to me?"

And I'd wish I could fly
in the star-speckled sky
and wash my face in a cloud,
and I'd sing to the moon
a silly sea tune till he
laughed and laughed out loud.

Then I'd land on a whale
with a black-and-white tail
who would rock me fast asleep,
and she'd carry me home
on a crest of foam
over the waters deep.

If I could live in a little house,
I'd live in a house by the sea.
An octopus would live next
door and take good care of me.

With an arm doing this,
and an arm doing that,
he'd cook and make my bed.
He'd sweep the floor and paint
my walls
and wash the clothes and
answer calls
and bake me chocolate bread.

I'd read him stories
while he worked
and serve him seaweed tea,
and I would thank him very
much for taking care of me.

If I could live in a little house,
I'd live in a house by the sea.
Some days I'd catch the sea in
a pail.
Some days the sea would
catch me!
I'd be wet, wet, wet
from my nose to my toes,
bobbing away from the shore
till the sea changed its mind

and carried me back
and tossed me alongside
my door.

When I can live in a little house,
I'll live in a house by the sea.
And I'll play in the sand,
dancing hand in hand
with a crab who is fond of me.

We'll play crab games
and trade our names,
so if you come calling me,
she'll hold out a claw
to shake your paw
as friendly as she can be.

Just ask the way
to the *crab* by the bay

and she'll point
the path to *me*.

Whenever you come
to the little house
that sits at the edge of the sea,
if you like, we can play
in the sand all day
a crab game, or two, or three.

And I'll call you, *Me*,
and you'll call me, *You*,
and no one will know
who is who
but us two
as we dance
round the rim
of the sea.

SING A SONG

OF SIXPENCE

Sing a song of sixpence,
A pocket full of rye;
Four-and-twenty blackbirds
Baked in a pie!

When the pie was opened,
The birds began to sing;
Wasn't that a dainty dish
To set before the king?

MARY WORE HER RED DRESS

Ma-ry wore her red dress, Red dress, red dress,

Ma-ry wore her red dress All day long.

Collected, adapted, and arranged by John A. Lomax and Alan Lomax.

THIS IS THE WAY WE GO TO SCHOOL

This is the way we go to school, go to school, go to school. This is the way we go to school, so early in the morning.

The Mulberry Bush

Here we go round the mulberry bush,
the mulberry bush, the mulberry bush.
Here we go round the mulberry bush,
on a cold and frosty morning.

BUENOS DÍAS, GOOD MORNING

Bue - nos dí - as, bue - nos dí - as, ¿có - mo es - tás? ¿có - mo es -

tás? Muy_bien,_ gra - cias, muy_bien,_ gra - cias, ¿y us - ted? ¿y us - ted?

Good morning, good morning,
How are you? How are you?
Very well, I thank you,

Very well, I thank you,
How about you? How about you?

If You're Happy and You Know It

If you're hap - py and you know it, clap your hands! (clap!) (clap!)

If you're hap - py and you know it, clap your hands! (clap!) (clap!)

If you're hap - py and you know it, and you real - ly want to show it

If you're hap - py and you know it, clap your hands! (clap!) (clap!)

If you're hap-py and you know it, stomp your feet! (stomp!) (stomp!)
If you're hap-py and you know it, shout Hoo-ray! (HOO-) (RAY!)

Loop de Loo

Lively

F

Here we go loop de loo,

F

Here we go loop de

C7 **F**

la, Here we go loop de loo,

C7 **F** **F**

all on a Sat-ur-day night._____ I put my right hand

F **C7**

in,_____ I put my right hand out,_____ I

F **C7** **F**

give my right hand a shake, shake, shake and turn___ my bo-dy a-bout.

I put my left hand in, *etc.*
I put my right foot in, *etc.*
I put my whole self in, *etc.*

123
SONGS

BINGO

Gaily

G

There was a farm - er had a dog, And Bin - go was his

C G Em D

name, O! B - I - N - G - O, B - I - N - G - O,

G Em C D G

B - I - N - G - O, and Bin - go was his name, O!

Em Am D7 G

BOUGHT ME A CAT

Fast

1. Bought me a cat, the cat pleased me, Fed my cat un-der yon-ders tree,
Cat went fid-dle - i - fee, fid-dle - i - fee.

2. Bought me a hen, the hen pleased me, Fed my hen un-der yon-ders tree,
Hen went chip-sy chop-sy, Cat went fid-dle-i - fee, fid-dle - i - fee.

3. Bought me a duck, the duck pleased me, Fed my duck un-der yon-ders tree.
Duck went slish- y slosh- y.
Hen went chip-sy chop-sy, Cat went fid-dle-i - fee, fid-dle-i - fee.

Bought me a goose, . . . Goose went qua, . . .
Bought me a dog, . . . Dog went boo, . . .
Bought me a sheep, . . . Sheep went baa, . . .
Bought me a cow, . . . Cow went moo, . . .
Bought me a horse, . . .
Horse went neigh, . . .

HEAD, SHOULDERS, KNEES, AND TOES

Head,   shoul-ders, knees and toes,   knees   and toes.

Head,   shoul-ders, knees and toes,   knees   and to - o - oes   and

Eyes   and   ears   and   mouth____ and____ nose.

Head,   shoul-ders, knees and toes,   knees   and toes.

(Chorus) And he played up-on a la-dle, a la-dle, he played up-on a
la-dle, a la-dle, and his name was Ai-ken Drum.

And his head was made of broccoli, *etc.*
And his nose was made of swiss cheese, *etc.*

You'll Sing a Song and I'll Sing a Song

by Ella Jenkins

You'll sing a song and I'll sing a song, Then we'll sing a song to-geth-er.

You'll sing a song and I'll sing a song in warm or win-try wea-ther.

EVERYTHING GROWS

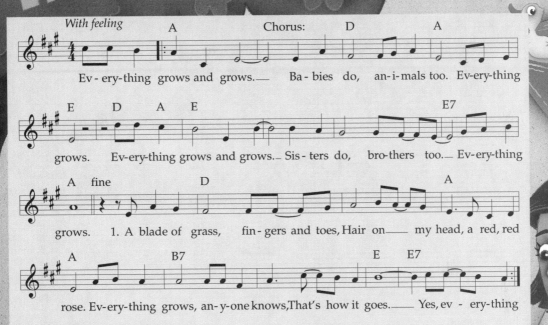

With feeling

A   Chorus: D   A

Ev - ery-thing grows and grows.— Ba - bies do, an-i-mals too. Ev-ery-thing

E   D   A   E   E7

grows.   Ev-ery-thing grows and grows.— Sis - ters do,   bro-thers too.— Ev-ery-thing

A   fine   D   A

grows.   1. A blade of grass,   fin - gers and toes, Hair on— my head, a red, red

A   B7   E   E7

rose. Ev-ery-thing grows, an - y-one knows, That's how it goes.— Yes, ev - ery-thing

2. Food on the farm, fish in the sea,
   Birds in the air, leaves on the tree.
   Everything grows, anyone knows,
   That's how it goes.

3. That's how it goes, under the sun.
   That's how it goes, under the rain.
   Everything grows, anyone knows.
   That's how it goes.

The Elephants

Moderately

One e - le - phant went out to___ play___
Un e - le - fan - te se ba - lan - ce - a - ba

Out on a spi - der web___ one day.
so - bre la te - la de u - na a - ra - ña,

She had___ such e - nor - mous___ fun, She
y co - mo és - ta no se rom - pí - a,

called for a - no - ther e - le - phant to come.
fue a lla - mar a o - tro e - le - fan - te.

Down by the Bay

Traditional

Down by the bay, where the wa-ter-mel-ons grow.

Back to my home I dare not go.

For if I do my mo-ther will say, "Did you

ev-er see a goose kiss-ing a moose, Down by the bay."

2. "Did you ever see a whale with a polka-dot tail . . ."

3. "Did you ever see a fly wearing a tie . . ."

4. "Did you ever see a bear combing his hair . . ."

5. "Did you ever see llamas eating their pajamas . . ."

6. "Did you ever have a time when you couldn't make a rhyme, Down by the bay."

Kookaburra

1. Koo - ka - bur - ra sits in the old gum tree,_____
2. Koo - ka - bur - ra sits in the old gum tree,_____

Mer - ry, mer - ry king of the bush is he._____
Count-ing all the kang - a - roos he can see._____

Laugh Koo - ka - bur - ra, laugh Koo - ka - bur - ra,
Watch Koo - ka - bur - ra, watch Koo - ka - bur - ra,

Gay your life must be.
Count - ing one, two, three.

The Bear Went over the Mountain

The bear went o-ver the moun - tain, The bear went o-ver the

moun - tain, The bear went o-ver the moun - tain, To see what he could

see._____ To see what he could see,_____ To see what he could

see_____ The oth - er side of the moun - tain, The oth - er side of the

moun-tain, The oth - er side of the moun - tain Was all__ that he_could see.

ALL WORK TOGETHER

Verse: D7

Woody Guthrie

My mom - my told___ me an' the teach-er told me, too,___ there's

all kinds of work that I can do: dry my dish-es,

sweep my floor, but if we all work to-geth-er it won't take ve - ry

long. Chorus: We all work to-geth-er with a wig-gle and a gig-gle, we

all work to - geth - er with a gig - gle and a grin. We

all work to - geth - er with a wig - gle and a gig - gle, we

all work to - geth - er with a gig - gle and a grin.

After Last Chorus:

With a wig - gle and a gig - gle and a goo - gle and a woo - gle and a

(2nd time)

jig - ger and a jag - ger and a gig - gle and a grin.

THE BUS SONG

The peo-ple in the bus go up and down, Up and down, up and down. The peo-ple in the bus go up and down, All a-round the town.

The wiper on the bus goes "Swish, swish, swish," *etc*.
The brake on the bus goes "Roomp, roomp roomp," *etc*.
The money on the bus goes "Clink, clink, clink," *etc*.

OLD MACDONALD HAD A FARM

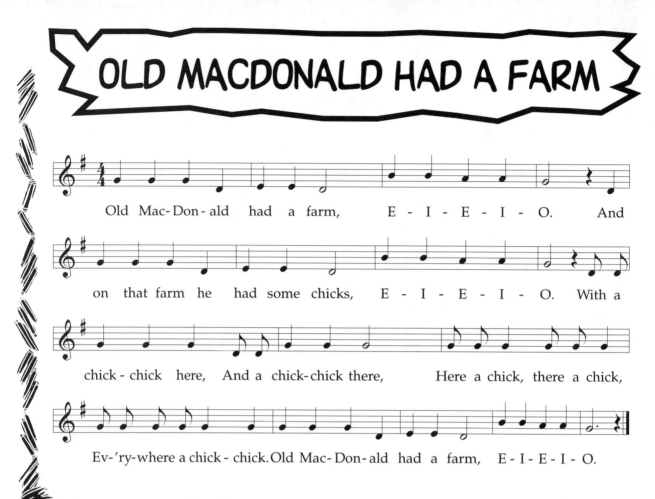

Old Mac-Don-ald had a farm, E - I - E - I - O. And

on that farm he had some chicks, E - I - E - I - O. With a

chick - chick here, And a chick-chick there, Here a chick, there a chick,

Ev-'ry-where a chick - chick. Old Mac-Don-ald had a farm, E - I - E - I - O.

Old MacDonald had a farm,
E-I-E-I-O.
And on that farm he had some ducks,
E-I-E-I-O.
With a quack-quack here,
And a quack-quack there,
Here a quack, there a quack,
Ev-'rywhere a quack-quack,
Chick-chick here,
Chick-chick there,
Here a chick, there a chick,
Ev-'rywhere a chick-chick,
Old MacDonald had a farm,
E-I-E-I-O.

Wild Geese

Calmly, but not too slowly

a Japanese folk song

Wild geese, wild geese, fly a - way!

Big goose a-head as you lead the way; Small geese be-hind as you

fly a - way. Peace - ful - ly, peace - ful - ly fly a - way!

The Farmer in the Dell

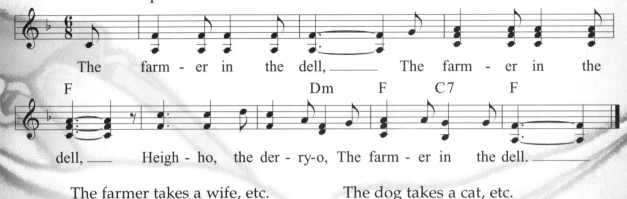

The farm-er in the dell, _____ The farm-er in the
dell, _____ Heigh-ho, the der-ry-o, The farm-er in the dell. _____

The farmer takes a wife, etc.
The wife takes a child, etc.
The child takes a nurse, etc.
The nurse takes a dog, etc.

The dog takes a cat, etc.
The cat takes a rat, etc.
The rat takes the cheese, etc.
The cheese stands alone, etc.

Old Mister Rabbit
An African American Folk Song

Old Mis-ter Rab-bit, you've got a might-y hab-it,

Of jump-ing in my gar-den and eat-ing all my cab-bage.

Eency Weency Spider

The een-cy ween-cy spi - der went up the wa - ter spout;____ Down came the rain and washed the spi - der out;____ Out came the sun and dried up all the rain, And the een-cy ween-cy spi - der went up the spout a - gain.____

The Ants Came Marching

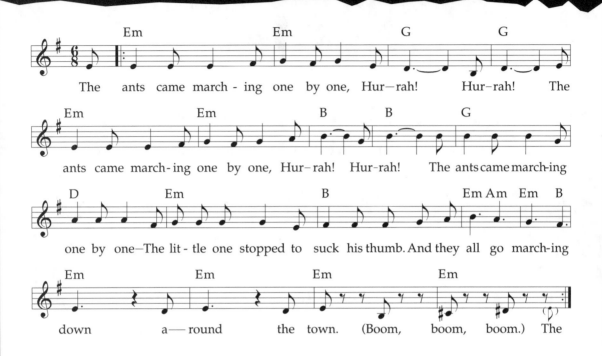

The ants came marching one by one, Hur—rah! Hur—rah! The
ants came march-ing one by one, Hur—rah! Hur—rah! The ants came march-ing
one by one—The lit-tle one stopped to suck his thumb. And they all go march-ing
down a—round the town. (Boom, boom, boom.) The

The ants came marching two by two . . .
The little one stopped to tie his shoe . . .

The ants came marching three by three . . .
The little one stopped to climb a tree . . .

The ants came marching four by four . . .
The little one stopped to shut the door . . .

The ants came marching five by five . . .
The little one stopped to take a dive . . .

The ants came marching six by six . . .
The little one stopped to pick up sticks . . .

The ants came marching seven by seven . . .
The little one stopped to go to heaven . . .

The ants came marching eight by eight . . .
The little one stopped to shut the gate . . .

The ants came marching nine by nine . . .
The little one stopped to scratch
his spine . . .

The ants came marching
ten by ten . . .
The little one stopped to say
THE END.

There's a Hole
in the Middle of the Sea

1. There's a hole in the mid-dle of the sea,
There's a hole in the mid-dle of the sea,
There's a hole, There's a hole,
There's a hole in the mid-dle of the sea.

2. There's a log in the hole in the middle
of the sea . . .

3. There's a bump on the log in the hole
in the middle of the sea . . .

4. There's a frog on the bump on
the log in the hole
in the middle
of the sea . . .

Index